THE SHADOW

MERIT EWEKA

CHAPTER I

The Anxieties of Sir Charles

Like all really uncommon beauties, Hyacinth could only be adequately described by the most hackneyed phrases. Her eyes were authentically sapphire-coloured; brilliant, frank eyes, with a subtle mischief in them, softened by the most conciliating long eyelashes. Then, her mouth was really shaped like a Cupid's bow, and her teeth *were* dazzling; also she had a wealth of dense, soft, brown hair and a tall, sylphlike, slimly-rounded figure. Her features were delicately regular, and her hands and feet perfection. Her complexion was extremely fair, so she was not a brunette; some remote Spanish ancestor on her mother's side was, however, occasionally mentioned as an apology for a type and a supple grace sometimes complained of by people with white eyelashes as rather un- English. So many artistic young men had told her she was like La Gioconda, that when she first saw the original in the Louvre she was so disappointed that she thought she would never smile again.

About ten minutes after the pretty creature had gone out, Anne, who had kept her eyes steadily on the clock, looked out of the window, from which she could see a small brougham driving up. She called out into the hall—

'If that's Sir Charles Cannon, tell him Miss Verney is out, but I have a message for him.'

A minute later there entered a thin and distinguished-looking, grey-haired man of about forty-five, wearing a smile of such excessive cordiality that one felt it could only have been brought to his well-bred lips by acute disappointment. Anne did not take the smile literally, but began to explain away the blow.

'I'm so sorry,' she said apologetically. 'I'm afraid it's partly my fault. When she suddenly decided to go out with that little Mrs Ottley, she told me vaguely to telephone to you. But how on earth could I know where you were?'

'How indeed? It doesn't matter in the least, my dear Miss Yeo. I mean, it's most unfortunate, as I've just a little free time. Lady Cannon's gone to a matinée at the St James's. We had tickets for the first night, but of course she wouldn't use them then.

She preferred to go alone in the afternoon, because she detests the theatre, anyhow, and afternoon performances

give her a headache. And if she does a thing that's disagreeable to her, she likes to do it in the most painful possible way. She has a beautiful nature.'

Anne smiled, and passed him a little gold box. 'Have a

cigarette?' she suggested.

'Thanks—I'm not really in a bad temper. But why this relapse of devotion to little Mrs Ottley? And why are you and I suddenly treated with marked neglect?'

'Mrs Ottley,' said Anne, 'is one of those young women, rather bored with their husbands, who are the worst possible companions for Hyacinth. They put her off marrying.'

'Bored, is she? She didn't strike me so. A pleasant, bright girl. I suppose she amuses Hyacinth?'

'Yes; of course, she's not a dull old maid over forty, like me,' said Anne.

'No-one would believe that description of you,' said Sir Charles, with a bow that was courtly but absent. As a matter of fact, he did believe it, but it wasn't true.

'If dear little Mrs Ottley,' he continued, 'married in too great a hurry, far be it from me to reproach her. I married in a hurry myself—when Hyacinth was ten.'

'And when she was eighteen you were very sorry,' said Anne in her colourless voice.

'Don't let us go into that, Miss Yeo. Of course, Hyacinth is a beautiful— responsibility. People seem to think she ought to have gone on living with us when she left school. But how was it possible? Hyacinth said she intended to live for her art, and Lady Cannon couldn't stand the scent of oils.' He glanced round the large panelled-oak room in which not a picture was to be seen. The only indication of its having ever been meant for a studio was the north light, carefully obstructed (on the grounds of unbecomingness) by gently-tinted draperies of some fabric suggesting Liberty's. 'Life wasn't worth living, trying to keep the peace!'

'But you must have missed her?'

'Still, I prefer coming to see her here. And knowing she has you with her is, after all, everything.'

He looked a question.

'Yes, she has. I mean, she seems rather—absorbed again lately,' said Anne.

'Who is it?' he asked. 'I always feel so indiscreet and treacherous talking over her private affairs like this with you, though she tells me everything herself. I'm not sure it's the act of a simple, loyal, Christian English gentleman; in fact, I'm pretty certain it's not. I suppose that's why I enjoy it so much.'

'I daresay,' said Anne; 'but she wouldn't mind it.' 'What has

been happening?'

'Nothing interesting. Hazel Kerr came here the other day and brought with him a poem in bronze lacquer, as he called it. He read it aloud—the whole of it.'

'Good heavens! Poetry! Do people still do that sort of thing? I thought it had gone out years ago—when I was a young man.'

'Of course, so it has. But Hazel Kerr is out of date. Hyacinth says he's almost a classic.'

'His verses?'

'Oh no! His method. She says he's an interesting survival—he's walked straight out of another age—the nineties, you know. There were poets in those days.'

'Method! He was much too young then to have a style at all, surely!'

'That *was* the style. It was the right thing to be very young in the nineties. It isn't now.'

'It's not so easy now, for some of us,' murmured Sir Charles. 'But Hazel

keeps it up,' Anne answered.

Sir Charles laughed irritably. 'He keeps it up, does he? But he sits people out openly, that shows he's not really dangerous. One doesn't worry about Hazel. It's that young man who arrives when everybody's going, or goes before anyone else arrives, that's what I'm a little anxious about.'

'If you mean Cecil Reeve, Hyacinth says he doesn't like her.'

'I'm sorry to hear that. If anything will interest her, that will. Yet I don't know why I should mind. At any rate, he certainly isn't trying to marry her for interested reasons, as he's very well off—or perhaps for any reasons. I'm told he's clever, too.'

'His appearance is not against him either,' said Anne dryly; 'so what's the matter with him?'

'I don't know exactly. I think he's capable of playing with her.' 'Perhaps

he doesn't really appreciate her,' suggested Anne.

'Oh, yes, he does. He's a connoisseur—confound him! He appreciates her all right. But it's all for himself—not for her. By the way, I've heard his name mentioned with another woman's name. But I happen to know there's nothing in it.'

'Would you really like her to marry soon?' Anne asked.

'In her position it would be better, I suppose,' said her guardian, with obvious distaste to the idea.

'Has there ever been anyone that you thoroughly approved of?' asked Anne.

He shook his head.

'I rather doubt if there ever will be,' Anne said.

'She's so clever, so impulsive! She lives so much on her emotions. If she were disappointed—in that way—it would mean so much to her,' Sir Charles said.

'She does change rather often,' said Anne.

'Of course, she's never really known her own mind.' He took a letter out of his pocket. 'I came partly to show her a letter from Ella—my girl at school in Paris, you know. Hyacinth is so kind to her. She writes to me very confidentially. I hope she's being properly brought up!'

'Let me read it.' She

read—

'DARLING PAPA,

'I'm having heavenly fun at school. Last night there was a ball for Madame's birthday. A proper grown-up ball, and we all danced. The men weren't bad. I had a lovely Easter egg, a chocolate egg, and inside that another egg with chocolate in it, and inside that another egg with a dear little turquoise charm in it. One man said I was a blonde anglaise, and had a keepsake face; and another has taken the Prix de Rome, and is going to be a schoolmaster. There were no real ices. Come over and see me soon. It's such a long time to the holidays. Love to mother.

'Your loving,

'ELLA.'

'A curious letter—for her age,' said Ella's father, replacing it. 'I wish she were here. It seems a pity Lady Cannon can't stand the noise of practising—and so on. Well, perhaps it's for the best.' He got up. 'Miss Yeo, I must go and fetch Lady Cannon now, but I'll come back at half-past six for a few minutes—on my way to the club.'

'She's sure to be here then,' replied Anne consolingly; 'and do persuade her not to waste all her time being kind to Edith Ottley. It can't do any good. She'd better leave them alone.'

'Really, it's a very innocent amusement. I think you're overanxious.'

'It's only that I'm afraid she might get mixed up in—well, some domestic row.'

'Surely it can't be as bad as that! Why—is Mr Ottley in love with her?' he asked, smiling.

'Very much indeed,' said Anne.

'Oh, really, Miss Yeo!—and does Mrs Ottley know it?' 'No, nor

Hyacinth either. He doesn't know it himself.'

'Then if nobody knows it, it can't matter very much,' said Sir Charles, feeling vaguely uncomfortable all the same. Before he went he took up a portrait of Hyacinth in an Empire dress with laurel leaves in her hair. It was a beautiful portrait. Anne thought that from the way he looked at it, anyone could have guessed Lady Cannon had tight lips and wore a royal fringe.... They parted with great friendliness.

Anne's wooden, inexpressive countenance was a great comfort to Sir Charles, in some moods. Though she was clever enough, she did not

have that superfluity of sympathy and responsiveness that makes one go away regretting one has said so much, and disliking the other person for one's expansion. One never felt that she had understood too accurately, nor that one had given oneself away, nor been indiscreetly curious.... It was like talking to a chair. What a good sort Anne was!

CHAPTER II

Anne Yeo

'Would you like me to play to you a little?' Anne asked, when Hyacinth had returned and was sitting in the carved-oak chimney-corner, looking thoughtful and picturesque.

'Oh no, please don't! Besides, I know you can't'

'No, thank goodness!' exclaimed Anne. 'I know I'm useful and practical, and I don't mind that; but anyhow, I'm not cheerful, musical, and a perfect lady, in exchange for a comfortable home, am I?'

'No, indeed,' said Hyacinth fervently.

'No-one can speak of me as "that pleasant, cultivated creature who lives with Miss Verney," can they?'

'Not, at any rate, if they have any regard for truth,' said Hyacinth.

'I wish you wouldn't make me laugh. Why should I have a sense of humour? I sometimes think that all your friends imagine it's part of my duty to shriek with laughter at their wretched jokes. It wasn't in the contract. If I were pretty, my ambition would have been to be an adventuress; but an adventuress with no adventures would be a little flat. I might have the worst intentions, but I should never have the chance of carrying them out. So I try to be as much as possible like Thackeray's shabby companion in a dyed silk.'

'Is that why you wear a sackcloth blouse trimmed with ashes?' said Hyacinth, with curiosity.

'No, that's merely stinginess. It's my nature to be morbidly economical, though I know I needn't be. If I hadn't had £500 a year left me, I should never have been able to come and live here, and drop all my horrid relations. I enjoy appearing dependent and being a spectator, and I've absolutely given up all interest in my own affairs. In fact, I haven't got any. And I take the keenest interest in other people's—romances. Principally, of course, in yours.'

'I'm sure I don't want you to be so vicarious as all that—thanks awfully,' said Hyacinth. 'At any rate, don't dress like a skeleton at the feast tomorrow, if you don't mind. I've asked the little Ottleys to dinner—and, I want Charles to come.'

'Oh, of course, if you expect Cecil Reeve!—I suppose you do, as you haven't mentioned it—I'll put on my real clothes to do you credit.' She looked out of the window. 'Here's poor old Charles again. How he does dislike Lady Cannon!'

'What a shame, Anne! He's angelic to her.'

'That's what I meant,' said Anne, going out quickly.

'Charles, how nice of you to call and return your own visit the same day! It's like Royalty, isn't it? It reminds me of the young man who was asked to call again, and came back in half an hour,' said Hyacinth.

'I didn't quite see my way to waiting till Monday,' he answered. 'We're going away the end of the week. Janet says she needs a change.'

'It would be more of a change if you remained in town alone; at least, without Aunty.'

From the age of ten Hyacinth had resented having to call Lady Cannon by this endearing name. How a perfect stranger, by marrying her cousin, could become her aunt, was a mystery that she refused even to try to solve. It was well meant, no doubt; it was supposed to make her feel more at home—less of an orphan. But though she was obedient on this point, nothing would ever induce her to call her cousin by anything but his Christian name, with no qualification. Instinctively she felt that to call them 'Charles and Aunty', while annoying the intruder, kept her guardian in his proper place. What that was she did not specify.

'Well, can't you stay in London and come here, and be confided in and consulted? You know you like that better than boring yourself to death at Redlands.'

'Never mind that. How did you enjoy your drive?'

'Immensely, and I've asked both the little Ottleys to come to dinner tomorrow—one of those impulsive, unconsidered invitations that one regrets the second after. I must make up a little party. Will you come?'

'Perhaps, if I arranged to follow Janet to Redlands the next day, I might. Who did you say was the other man?'

'I expect Cecil Reeve,' she said. 'Don't put on that air of marble archness, Charles. It doesn't suit you at all. Tell me something about him.'

'I can't stand him. That's all I know about him,' said Sir Charles. 'Oh, is that

all? That's just jealousy, Charles.'

'Absurd! How can a married man, in your father's place, a hundred years older than you, be jealous?'

'It is wonderful, isn't it?' she said. 'But you must know something about him. You know everyone.'

'He's Lord Selsey's nephew—and his heir—if Selsey doesn't marry again. He's only a young man about town—the sort of good-looking ass that your sex admires.'

'Charles, what a brute you are! He's very clever.'

'My dear child, yes—as a matter of fact, I believe he is. Isn't he ever going to *do* something?'

'I don't know,' she said. 'I wish he would. Oh, *why* don't you like him?'

'What can it matter about me?' he answered. 'Why are you never satisfied unless I'm in love with the same people that you are?'

'Charles!' she exclaimed, standing up. 'Don't you understand that not a word, not a look has passed to suggest such a thing? I never met anyone so—'

'So cautious?'

'No, so listless, and so respectful; and yet so amusing…. But I'm pretty certain that he hates me. I wish I knew why.'

'And you hate him just as much, of course?'

'No, sometimes I don't. And then I want you to agree with me. No-one sympathises really so well as you, Charles.'

'Not even Miss Yeo?'

'No, I get on so well with Anne because she doesn't She's always interested, but I prefer her never to agree with me, as she lives here. It would be enervating to have someone always there and perpetually sympathetic. Anne is a tonic.'

'You need a little opposition to keep you up,' said Sir Charles.

'Didn't I once hear something about his being devoted to someone? Wasn't there a report that he was going to be married to a Mrs. Raymond?'

'I believe it was once contradicted in the *Morning Post* that he was engaged to her,' said Sir Charles. 'But I'm sure there's no truth in it. I know her.'

'No truth in the report? Or the contradiction?' 'In either.

In anything.'

'So you know her. What's she like?' Hyacinth asked anxiously.

'Oh, a dear, charming creature—you'd like her; but not pretty, nor young. About my age,' he said.

'Oh, I see! *That's* all right, then!' She clapped her hands.

'Well, I must go. I'll arrange to turn up to dinner tomorrow.' He took his hat, looking rather depressed.

'And try to make him like me!' she commanded, as Sir Charles took leave.

CHAPTER III

The Sound Sense of Lady Cannon

Lady Cannon had never been seen after half-past seven except in evening dress, generally a velvet dress of some dark crimson or bottle- green, so tightly-fitting as to give her an appearance of being rather upholstered than clothed. Her cloaks were always like well-hung curtains, her trains like heavy carpets; one might fancy that she got her gowns from Gillows. Her pearl dog-collar, her diamond ear-rings, her dark red fringe and the other details of her toilette were put on with the same precision when she dined alone with Sir Charles as if she were going to a ceremonious reception. She was a very tall, fine-looking woman. In Paris, where she sometimes went to see Ella at school, she attracted much public attention as *une femme superbe.* Frenchmen were heard to remark to one another that her husband *ne devrait pas s'embêter* (which, as a matter of fact, was precisely what he did—to extinction); and even in the streets when she walked out the gamins used to exclaim, '*Voilà l'Arc de Triomphe qui se promène!*'—to her intense fury and gratification. She was still handsome, with hard, wide-open blue eyes, and straight features. She always held her head as if she were being photographed in a tiara *en profil perdu*. It was in this attitude that she had often been photographed and was now most usually seen; and it seemed so characteristic that even her husband, if he accidentally caught a glimpse of her full-face, hastily altered his position to one whence he could behold her at right angles.

As she grew older, the profile in the photographs had become more and more *perdu*; the last one showed chiefly the back of her head, besides a basket of flowers, and a double staircase, leading (one hoped) at least to one of the upper rooms in Buckingham Palace.

Lady Cannon had a very exalted opinion of her own charms, virtues, brilliant gifts, and, above all, of her sound sense. Fortunately for her, she had married a man of extraordinary amiability, who had always taken every possible precaution to prevent her discovering that in this opinion she was practically alone in the world.

Having become engaged to her through a slight misunderstanding in a country house, Sir Charles had not had the courage to explain away the mistake. He decided to make the best of it, and did so the more easily as it was one of those so-called suitable matches that the friends and acquaintances of both parties approve of and desire far more than the parties concerned. A sensible woman was surely required at Redlands and in the London house, especially as Sir Charles had been left guardian and trustee to a pretty little heiress.

It had taken him a very short time to find out that the reputation for sound sense was, like most traditions, founded on a myth, and that if his wife's vanity was only equalled by her egotism, her most remarkable characteristic was her excessive silliness. But she loved him, and he kept his discovery to himself.

'Twenty-five minutes to eight!' she exclaimed, holding out a little jewelled watch, as Sir Charles came in after his visit to Hyacinth. 'And we have a new cook, and I specially, *most* specially told her to have dinner ready punctually at half-past seven! This world is indeed a place of trial!'

Sir Charles's natural air of command seemed to disappear in the presence of Lady Cannon. He murmured a graceful apology, saying he would not dress. Nothing annoyed, even shocked her more than to see her husband dining opposite her in a frock-coat. However, of two evils she chose the less. They went in to dinner.

'I haven't had the opportunity yet of telling you my opinion of the play this afternoon,' she said. 'I found it interesting, and I wonder I hadn't seen it before.'

'You sent back our stalls for the first night,' remarked Sir Charles.

'Certainly I did. I dislike seeing a play until I have seen in the papers whether it is a success or not.'

'Those newspaper fellows aren't always right,' said Sir Charles.

'Perhaps not, but at least they can tell you whether the thing is a success. I should be very sorry to be seen at a failure. Very sorry indeed.'

She paused, and then went on—

'*James Wade's Trouble* has been performed three hundred times, so it must be clever. In my opinion, it must have done an immense amount of harm—good, I mean. A play like that, so full of noble sentiments and high principles, is—to me—as good as a sermon!'

'Oh, is it? I'm sorry I couldn't go,' said Sir Charles, feeling very glad.

'I suppose it was the club, as usual, that made you late. Do you know, I have a great objection to clubs.'

He nodded sympathetically.

'That is to say, I thoroughly approve of your belonging to several. I'm quite aware that in your position it's the right thing to do, but I can't understand why you should ever go to them, having two houses of your own. And that reminds me, we are going down to Redlands tomorrow, are we not? I've had a little' (she lowered her voice) 'lumbago; a mere passing touch, that's all—and the change will cure me. I think you neglect Redlands, Charles. You seem to me to regard your responsibilities as a landowner with indifference bordering on aversion. You never seem amused down there—unless we have friends.'

'We'll go tomorrow if you like,' said he. 'That's

satisfactory.'

'I can easily put off the Duke,' he said thoughtfully, as he poured out more wine.

She sprang up like a startled hare.

'Put off the … what are you talking about?'

'Oh, nothing. The Duke of St Leonard's is giving a dinner at the club tomorrow, and I was going. But I can arrange to get out of it.'

'Charles! I never heard of anything so absurd! You must certainly go to the dinner. How like you! How casual of you! For a mere trifle to offend the man who might be of the greatest use to you—politically.'

'Politically! What do you mean? And it isn't a trifle when you've set your mind on going away tomorrow. I know you hate to change your plans, my dear.'

'Certainly I do, but I shall not change my plans. I shall go down tomorrow, and you can join me on Friday.'

'Oh, I don't think I'll do that,' said Sir Charles, rather half-heartedly. 'Why should you take the journey alone?'

'But I shall not be alone. I shall have Danvers with me. You need have no anxiety. I beg of you, I *insist*, that you stay, and go to this dinner.'

'Well, of course, if you make a point of it—'

She smiled, well pleased at having got her own way, as she supposed. 'That's right,

Charles. Then you'll come down on Friday.'

'By the early train,' said Sir Charles.

'No, I should suggest your coming by the later train. It's more convenient to meet you at the station.'

'Very well—as you like,' said he, inwardly a little astonished, as always, at the easy working of the simple old plan, suggesting what one does not wish to do in order to be persuaded into what one does.

'And, by the way, I haven't heard you speak of Hyacinth lately. You had better go and see her. A little while ago you were always wasting your time about her, and I spoke to you about it, Charles—I think?'

'I think you did,' said he.

'But, though at one time I was growing simply tired of her name, I didn't mean that you need not look after her at *all*. Go and see her, and explain to her I can't possibly accompany you. Tell her I've got chronic lumbago very badly indeed, and I'm obliged to go to the country, but I shall certainly make a point of calling on her when I return. You won't forget, Charles?'

'Certainly not.'

'I should go oftener,' she continued apologetically, 'but I have such a great dislike to that companion of hers. I think Miss Yeo a most unpleasant person.'

'She isn't really,' said Sir Charles.

'I do wish we could get Hyacinth married,' said Lady Cannon. 'I know what a relief it would be to you, and it seems to me such an unheard-of thing for a young girl like that to be living practically alone!'

'We've been through that before, Janet. Remember, there was nothing else to do unless she continued to live with us. And as your nerves can't even stand Ella—'

Lady Cannon dropped the point.

'Well, we must get her married,' she said again. 'What a good thing Ella is still so young! Girls are a dreadful responsibility,' and she swept graciously from the dining-room.

Sir Charles took out an irritating little notebook of red leather, the sort of thing that is advertised when lost as 'of no value to anyone but the owner.' It was full of mysterious little marks and unintelligible little notes. He put down, in cabalistic signs, '*Hyacinth's dinner, eight o'clock.*' He enjoyed writing her name, even in hieroglyphics.

CHAPTER IV

A Proposal

'I say, Eugenia.' 'Well, Cecil?'

'Look here, Eugenia.' 'What is it, Cecil?' 'Will you marry me?' 'I beg your pardon?'

'Will you many me, Eugenia?'

'What?'

'You heard what I said. I asked you to marry me. Will you?'

'*Certainly* not! Most decidedly not! How can you ask such a ridiculous question!'

The lady who thus scornfully rejected a proposal was no longer young, and had never been beautiful. In what exactly her attraction consisted was perhaps a mystery to many of those who found themselves under the charm. Her voice and smile were very agreeable, and she had a graceful figure. If she looked nearly ten years younger than her age (which was forty-four), this was in no way owing to any artificial aid, but to a kind of brilliant vitality, not a bouncing mature liveliness, but a vivid, intense, humorous interest in life that was and would always remain absolutely fresh. She was naturalness itself, and seemed unconscious or careless of her appearance. Nor did she have that well-preserved air of so many modern women who seem younger than their years, but seemed merely clever, amiable, very unaffected, and rather ill. She had long, veiled- looking brown eyes, turned up at the corners, which gave to her glance an amusing slyness. It was a very misleading physiognomical effect, for she was really unusually frank. She wore a dull grey dress that was neither artistic, becoming, nor smart. In fact, she was too charming to be dowdy, and too careless to be chic; she might have been a great celebrity.

The young man who made the suggestion above recorded was fair and clean-shaven, tall and well-made, with clear-cut feature; in fact, he was

very good-looking—good-looking as almost only an Englishman can be. Under a reserved, dandified manner, he tried unsuccessfully to conceal the fact that he was too intelligent for his type. He did not, however, quite attain his standard of entire expressionlessness; and his bright, light-blue eyes and fully-curved lips showed the generous and emotional nature of their owner. At this moment he seemed very much out of temper.

They were sitting in a dismal little drawing-room in one of the smallest houses in a dreary street in Belgravia. The room was crowded with dateless, unmeaning furniture, and disfigured by muddled, mistaken decoration. Its designer, probably, had meant well, but had been very far from carrying out his meaning. There were too many things in the room, and most of them were wrong. It would be unjust, however, to suppose Mrs Raymond did not know this. Want of means, and indifference, or perhaps perverseness, had caused her to leave the house unchanged since his death as a sort of monument to poor Colonel Raymond's erring taste.

'You might just as well marry me as not,' said Cecil, in his level voice, but with pleading eyes. He made the gesture of trying to take her hand, but she took hers away.

'You are very pressing, Cecil, but I think not. You know perfectly well—I'm sure I make no secret of it—that I'm ten years older than you. Old enough to be your mother! Am I the sort of person who would take advantage of the fancy of a gilded youth? And, now I come to think of it, your proposal's quite insulting. It's treating me like an adventuress! It's implying that you think I *would* marry you! Apologise, and withdraw it at once, or I'll never speak to you again.'

'This is nonsense. To begin with,' said Cecil, 'I may be a little gilded—not so very—but I'm far from being a youth. I'm thirty-four.'

'Yes, I know! That's just the absurd part,' she answered inconsequently. 'It's not as if you were a mere boy and didn't know better! And you know how I *hate* this sort of thing.'

'I know you do, and very likely I wouldn't have worried about marrying at all if you had been nicer to me—in other ways. You see, you brought it on yourself!'

'What *do* you mean? I *am* nice. Don't you come here whenever you like— or nearly? Didn't I dine with you once—a year or two ago? I forget, but I think I did.'

'You never did,' he answered sharply.

'Then it must have been with somebody else. Of course I didn't. I shouldn't dream of such a thing.'

'Someone else! Yes, of course; that's it. Well, I want you to marry me, Eugenia, because I want to get you away from everyone else. You see my point?'

She laughed. 'Oh, jealousy! That's the last straw. Do you know that you're a nuisance, Cecil?'

'Because I love you?' he said, trying to look into her sly Japanese eyes. She avoided

his glance.

'Because you keep on bothering. Always writing, always telephoning, always calling! As soon as I've disposed of *one* invitation or excuse to meet, you invent another. But this last idea is quite too exasperating.' She spoke more gently. 'Don't you know, Cecil, that I've been a widow for years? Would I be so ridiculous as to marry again? Why, the one thing I can't stand is being interfered with! I prefer, far prefer, being poor and alone to that. Now what I want you to do is to marry someone else. I have an idea who I should like it to be, but I won't talk about it now. It's the most charming girl in the world. I shan't tell you her name, that would be tactless. It's that lovely Miss Verney, of course. She's much too good for you—an heiress, a beauty, and an orphan! But she's wonderful; and she really deserves you.'

He stopped her.

'How heartless you are!' he said admiringly.

'Really not, Cecil. I'm very fond of you. I'd be your best friend if you'd let me, but I shan't speak to you again or receive you at all unless you promise not to repeat that nonsense about marrying. I know how horridly obstinate you are! Please remember it's out of the question.'

At this moment the servant brought in a letter to Mrs Raymond. As she read it, Cecil thought she changed colour.

'It's only a line from Sir Charles Cannon,' she said. 'What's he

writing about?'

'Really, Cecil! What right have you to ask? I certainly shan't say. It's about his ward, if you must know. And now I think you'd better go, if you will make these violent scenes.'

He stood up.

'You must let me come soon again,' he said rather dejectedly. 'I'll try not to come tomorrow. Shall I?'

'Yes, do try—not to come, I mean. And will you do everything I tell you?'

'I suppose it will please you if I dine with Hyacinth Verney this evening? She asked me yesterday. I said I was half-engaged, but would let her know.'

'Yes, it *would* please me very much indeed,' said Mrs Raymond. 'Please do it, and try to know her better. She's sweet. I don't know her, but—'

'All right. If you'll be nice to me. Will you?'

She was reading the letter again, and did not answer when he said good-bye and left the room.

CHAPTER V

The Little Ottleys

'Edith, I want you to look nice tonight, dear; what are you going to wear?' 'My Other

Dress,' said Edith.

'Is it all right?'

'It ought to be. Would you like to know what I've done to it? I've cut the point into a square, and taken four yards out of the skirt; the chiffon off my wedding-dress has been made into kimono sleeves; then I'm going to wear my wedding-veil as a sort of scarf thrown carelessly over the shoulders; and I've turned the pointed waist-band round, so that it's quite *right* and short-waisted at the back now, and—'

'Oh, don't tell me the horrible details! I think you might take a little interest in *me*. I thought of wearing a buttonhole. Though you may have forgotten it now, before I was a dull old married man, I was supposed to dress rather well, Edith.'

'I know you were.'

'I thought I'd wear a white carnation.'

'I should wear two—one each side. It would be more striking.'

'That's right! Make fun of me! I hope you'll be ready in time. They dine at eight, you know.'

'Bruce, you're not going to begin to dress yet, are you? It's only just four.' He

pretended not to hear, and said peevishly—

'I suppose they don't expect *us* to ask *them*? I daresay it's well known we can't return all the hospitality we receive.'

'I daresay it is.'

'It's awful not having a valet,' said Bruce.

'But it would be more awful if we had,' said Edith. 'Where on earth could we put him—except in the bathroom?'

'I don't think you'll look you're best tonight,' he answered rather revengefully.

'Give me a chancel Wait till I've waved my hair!'

He read the paper for a little while, occasionally reading aloud portions of it that she had already read, then complained that she took no interest in public events.

'What do you think Archie brought home today,' she said to change the subject, 'in his Noah's Ark? Two snails!' She laughed.

'Revolting! *I* don't know where he gets his tastes from. Not from *my* family, that I'm quite sure.' He yawned ostentatiously.

'I think I shall have a rest,' Bruce said presently. 'I had a very bad night last night. I scarcely slept at all.'

'Poor boy!' Edith said kindly. She was accustomed to the convention of Bruce's insomnia, and it would never have occurred to her to appear surprised when he said he hadn't closed his eyes, though she happened to know there was no cause for anxiety. If he woke up ten minutes before he was called, he thought he had been awake all night; if he didn't he saw symptoms of the sleeping sickness.

She arranged cushions on the sofa and pulled the blinds down. A minute later he turned on the electric light and began to read again. Then he turned it out, pulled up the blinds, and called her back.

'I want to speak to you about my friend Raggett,' he said seriously. 'I've asked him to dinner here tomorrow. What shall we have?'

'Oh, Bruce! Let's wait and settle tomorrow.'

'You don't know Raggett, but I think you'll like him. I *think* you will. In any case, there's no doubt Raggett's been remarkably decent to me. In fact, he's a very good sort.'

'Fancy!' said Edith.

'Why do you say fancy?' he asked irritably.

'I don't exactly know. I must say something. I'm sure he's nice if he's a friend of yours, dear.'

'He's a clever chap in his way. At least, when I say clever, I don't mean clever in the ordinary sense.'

'Oh, I see,' said Edith.

'He's very amusing,' continued Bruce. 'He said a very funny thing to me the other day. Very funny indeed. It's no use repeating it, because unless you knew all the circumstances and the *characters* of the people that he told the story of, you wouldn't see the point. Perhaps, after all, I'd better ask him to dine at the club.'

'Oh no! Let him come here. Don't you think I'm worthy to see Raggett?'

'Oh nonsense, dear, I'm very proud of you,' said Bruce kindly. 'It isn't exactly that.... Mind you, Raggett's quite a man of the world—and yet he *isn't* a man of the world, if you know what I mean.'

'I see,' said Edith again.

'I can't decide whether to ask him here or not,' said Bruce, walking up and down the room in agitation.

'Well, suppose we leave it till tomorrow. You can make up your mind then,' she said good-naturedly.

Edith was dressed, when she found Bruce still in the throes of an agitated toilet. Having lost his collar-stud, he sat down and gave himself up to cold despair.

'You go without me,' he said in a resigned voice. 'Explain the reason—no, don't explain it. Say I've got influenza—but then perhaps they'll think you ought to look after me, and—'

'Here it is!' said Edith.

In the cab he recovered suddenly, and told her she looked awfully pretty, which cheered her very much. She was feeling rather tired. She had spent several hours in the nursery that day, pretending to be a baby giraffe with so much success that Archie had insisted upon countless encores, until, like all artists who have to repeat the same part too often, she felt the performance was becoming mechanical.

CHAPTER VI

Hyacinth's Little Dinner

'The little Ottleys,' as they were called (they were a tall, fine-looking couple), found themselves in a small circle of people who were all most pleasing to the eye, with the single exception of Miss Yeo. And even she, in a markedly elegant dress of a peculiarly vicious shade of green, had her value in the picture. A little shocked by the harshness of the colour, one's glance turned with relief to Hyacinth, in satin of a blue so pale that it looked like the reflection of the sky in water. A broad, pale blue ribbon was wound in and out of her brown hair in the Romney fashion. Of course she looked her best. Women always do if they wish to please one man when others are there, and she was in the slightly exalted frame of mind that her reflection in the mirror had naturally given her.

The faint atmosphere of chaperonage that always hung about Sir Charles in Hyacinth's house did not interfere with his personal air of enjoying an escapade, nor with his looking distinguished to the very verge of absurdity. As to Cecil, the reaction from his disappointment of the afternoon had made him look more vivid than usual. He was flushed with failure.

He talked rather irresponsibly, and looked at Hyacinth, his neighbour at dinner, with such obvious appreciation, that her gaiety became infectious. In the little panelled dining-room which, like all the house, was neither commonplace nor bizarre, but simple and distinguished, floated an atmosphere of delightful ease and intimacy.

Sir Charles admired the red roses, which Anne declared she had bought for two-and-threepence.

'Very ingenious,' said Sir Charles.

'I *am* ingenious and clever,' said Anne. 'I get my cleverness from my father, and my economy from my mother. My father's a clergyman, but his wife was a little country girl—a sort of Merry Peasant; like Schumann's piece, you know. Peasants are always merry.'

'I fancy that's a myth,' said Cecil. 'If not, I've been singularly unfortunate, for all the peasants *I* ever ran across seemed most depressed.'

'Of course, if you ran over them!' said Hyacinth.

'But I didn't exactly run over them; I only asked them the way to somewhere. They *were* angry! Now I come to think of it, though, they weren't peasants at all. It was only one man. He was a shepherd. I got to know him better afterwards, and he was rather a good chap. Shepherds don't have a bad time; they just wear ribbons and crooks and dance with shepherdesses, you know.'

'Oh, then *can* you tell me why a red sky at night is a shepherd's delight?' asked Hyacinth. 'Is it because it's a sign of rain, and he needn't look after the sheep, but can go fast asleep like little Bo-peep—or was it little Boy Blue—if he likes?'

'For you, I'll try to find out; but I'm ashamed to say I know very little of natural history—or machinery, or lots of other interesting things. And, what's far worse, I don't even want to know any more. I like to think there are some mysteries left in life.'

'I quite agree with you that it would be rather horrid to know exactly how electricity works, and how trains go, and all that sort of thing. I like some things just to *happen*. I never broke my dolls to see what they were made of. I had them taken away the *moment* any sawdust began to come out,' said Hyacinth.

'You were perfectly right, Miss Verney. You're an Idealist; at least, you don't like practical details. But still you take a great interest in other people psychologically. You want to know, I'm sure, just how a shepherd really feels, and why he feels it. I don't even care for that, and I'm not very keen on scenery, or places either, or even things. My Uncle Ted's so frightfully fond of Things. He's a collector, you know, and I don't sympathise a bit. In fact, I hate things.'

'You seem rather difficult to please, Mr Reeve. What do you like?' 'People; at

least, some people. Don't you?'

'Do you like people who talk nonsense?'

'Yes, and still more people who listen to it charmingly,' he answered. 'I didn't know before tonight that you ever listened to nonsense or
talked it. I always thought you were the person who solves all the Hard Cases in *Vanity Fair*—under different names.'

'I wonder you didn't think I won all the prizes in the Limericks,' said Hyacinth.

'I have my faults, Miss Verney, but I'm not blasphemous. Will you have an olive?'

She accepted it. He lowered his voice to say— 'How

wonderful you're looking tonight!'

'What am I to say to that? I don't think people should make unanswerable remarks at dinner,' she said, trying to look reproving, but turning pink with pleasure.

'If people will look adorable at dinner—or anywhere—they must take the consequences,' said Cecil, under cover of a very animated discussion between Bruce and Miss Yeo on sixpenny cab-fares.

Then for a second he felt a remorseful twinge of disloyalty. But that was nonsense; wasn't he obeying Mrs Raymond's distinct commands? Nothing would please her so much....

And to flirt with Hyacinth was not at all a disagreeable task. He reflected that Eugenia might have asked him to do something a good deal harder.

Under the combined influence, then, of duty, pique, and a little champagne, he gave way to the curious fascination that Hyacinth had always had for him, and she was only too ready to be happy.

He remembered how he had first met her. He had been dragged to the Burlingtons' dance—he loathed all large parties—and, looking drearily round, he'd been struck by, and asked to be introduced to, Miss Verney. She wasn't Eugenia, of course, and could never, he was sure, be part of his life. He thought that Eugenia appealed to his better nature and to his intellect.

He felt even a little ashamed of the purely sensuous attraction Hyacinth possessed for him, while he was secretly very proud of being in love with Mrs Raymond. Not everyone would appreciate Eugenia! Cecil was still young enough to wish to be different from other people, while desiring still more, like all Englishmen, to *appear* as much as possible like everybody else.

He did not thoroughly understand Hyacinth; he couldn't quite place her. She was certainly not the colourless *jeune fille* idealised by the French,

but she had even less of the hard abruptness of the ordinary young unmarried Englishwoman. She called herself a bachelor girl, but hadn't the touch of the Bohemian that phrase usually seems to imply. She was too plastic, too finished. He admired her social dexterity, her perfect harmony with the charming background she had so well arranged for herself. Yet, he thought, for such a young girl, only twenty-two, she was too complex, too civilised. Mrs Raymond, for instance, seemed much more downright and careless. He was growing somewhat bewildered between his analysis of her character and his admiration for her mouth, an admiration that was rather difficult to keep entirely cool and theoretical, and that he felt a strong inclination to show in some more practical manner.... With a sigh he turned to Edith Ottley, his other neighbour.

As soon as Anne had locked up she removed with the greatest care her emerald dress, which she grudged wearing a second longer than was necessary, and put on an extraordinary dressing-gown, of which it was hardly too much to say that there was probably not another one exactly like it in Europe. Hyacinth always said it had been made out of an old curtain from the Rev Mr Yeo's library in the Devonshire Rectory, and Anne did not deny it.

She then screwed up her hair into a tight knot, put one small piece of it into a curling pin, which she then pinned far back on her head (as if afraid that the effect on the forehead would be too becoming), took off her dainty green shoes, put on an enormous pair of grotesque slippers, carpet slippers (also a relic), and went into Hyacinth's room. Anne made it a rule every evening to go in for a few minutes to see Hyacinth and talk against everyone they had seen during the day. She seemed to regard it as a sacred duty, almost like saying her prayers. Hyacinth sometimes professed to find this custom a nuisance, but she would certainly have missed it. Tonight she was smiling happily to herself, and took no notice of Anne's entrance.

'I suppose you think it went off well,' said Anne aggressively. 'Didn't it?'

'I thought the dinner was ridiculous. A young girl like you asking two or three friends needn't have a banquet fit for a Colonial Conference. Besides, the cook lost her head. She sent up the same dish twice.'

'Did she? How funny! How was that?'

'Of course, *you* wouldn't know. She and the kitchenmaid were playing Diabolo till the last minute in the housekeeper's room. However, you needn't worry; nobody noticed it.'

'That's all right. Didn't Edith look pretty?' Anne poked

the fire spitefully.

'Like the outside of a cheap chocolate-box.'

'Oh, Anne, what nonsense! Bruce seemed irritable, and fatuous. I didn't envy Edith going back with him.'

'Bruce was jealous of Cecil Reeve, of course. You hardly looked at anybody else.'

'Anne, really tonight there were one or two little things that made me think he is beginning to like me. I don't say he's perfect; I daresay he has his faults. But there's something I like about his face. I wonder what it is.'

'I know what it is, he's very good-looking,' said Anne. 'Do you

think he cares for me?'

'No, I don't.'

'Oh, Anne!'

'I think, perhaps, he will, in time—in a way.'

'Do you think if I were very careful not to show I liked him it would be better?'

'No, there's only one chance for you.' 'What is

it?'

'Keep on hammering.'

'*Indeed* I shan't! I never heard of such a thing. I suppose you think there's somebody else?' said Hyacinth, sitting up angrily.

'Oh, I daresay he's just finishing off with someone or other, and you may catch him on the rebound.'

'What horrid things you say!'

'I only say what I think,' said Anne. 'Anyhow, you had a success tonight, I could see, because poor Charles seemed so depressed. Why do you have all these electric lights burning when one lamp would be enough?'

'Oh, go away, Anne, and don't bother,' said Hyacinth, laughing.

On his return home, Cecil suddenly felt a violent reaction in favour of Mrs Raymond. Certainly he had enjoyed his evening with Hyacinth, but it was very bitter to him to think what pleasure that enjoyment would have given to Eugenia.... He began to think he couldn't live without her. Something must be done. Further efforts must be made. The idea struck him that he would go and see his uncle, Lord Selsey, about it. He knew Uncle Ted was really fond of him, and wouldn't like to see his life ruined (so he put it to himself), and his heart broken, though he also probably would disapprove from the worldly point of view. Decidedly unhappy, yet to a certain extent enjoying his misery, Cecil went to sleep.

CHAPTER VII

Lord Selsey

The mere thought of confiding in Lord Selsey was at once soothing and bracing. He was a widower with no children, and Cecil was by way of being his heir. Since the death of his wife he lived in a kind of cultured retirement in a large old house standing a little by itself in Cambridge Gate. He used to declare that this situation combined all the advantages of London and the country, also that the Park that was good enough for the Regent was good enough for him. He had a decided cult for George IV; and there was even more than a hint of Beau Brummel in his dress. The only ugly thing in the house was a large coloured print of the pavilion at Brighton.

In many ways Lord Selsey was Cecil's model; and unconsciously, in his uncle's suave presence, the young man's manner always became more expressive and his face more inscrutable.

Lord Selsey was remarkably handsome; the even profile, well-shaped head, and blond colouring were much the same in uncle and nephew, the uncle's face having, perhaps, a more idealistic cast. The twenty years' difference in age had only given the elder man a finer, fairer, more faded look, and the smooth light hair, still thick, was growing grey.

Cecil was not surprised to find his uncle sitting in his smoking-room, smoking, and not reading the morning paper. He was looking over his collection of old coins. At a glance he saw by Cecil's excessive quietness that the boy, as he called him, was perturbed, so he talked about the coins for some minutes.

Cecil made little attempt to conceal that fact that Things bored him. 'Well, what

is it?' said Lord Selsey abruptly.

Cecil couldn't think of anything better by way of introducing the trouble than the vaguely pessimistic statement that everything was rather rotten.

'You don't gamble, you're not even very hard up.... It's a woman, of course,' said Lord Selsey, 'and you want to marry, I suppose, or you wouldn't come to me about it.... Who is she?'

Cecil gave a rough yet iridescent sketch of Mrs Raymond.

'Of course she's older than I am, but it doesn't make the slightest difference. She's been a widow ever since she was twenty. She's very hard up, and she doesn't care. She's refused me, but I want to make her come round.... No, she isn't *pretty*, not very.'

Lord Selsey put his old coins away, and leant back in his chair. 'I should

like to see her,' he said thoughtfully.

'I'm sure of one thing, uncle you could never have any vulgar, commonplace ideas about her—I mean, she's so *peculiarly* disinterested, and all that sort of thing. You mustn't fancy she's a dangerous syren, don't you know, or.... For instance, she doesn't care much for dress; she just sticks up her hair anyhow, and parts it in the middle.'

'Then it would certainly be difficult to believe anything against her,' said Lord Selsey.

'Besides, she really wants me to marry someone else.' 'Who?'

'She's always trying to persuade me to propose to Hyacinth Verney ... you know, that pretty girl, old Cannon's ward.... She is awfully pretty, of course, I know.'

'I should like to see her,' said Lord Selsey.

Cecil smiled. It was well known that Lord Selsey was a collector. Though no-one could have less of the pompous, fatuous vanity of the Don Juan, beauty had always played, and always would play, a very prominent part in his life. It was, in fact, without exception, his greatest pleasure, and interest—even passion. The temperament that gave to beauty and charm a rather inordinate value had, no doubt, descended to his nephew. But Cecil was, in that as in everything else, much less of a dilettante.

'You actually want me to advise you to persuade Mrs Raymond to marry you? My dear boy, how can I?'

'How is it you don't say she's quite right not to?' asked Cecil curiously.

'From her point of view I think she's quite wrong. As you're both practically free and you would marry her tomorrow—or this afternoon for choice—if she cared for you she would probably do it. Where I think she's wrong is in not caring for you.... Who is it?'

'I don't believe it's anyone. Eugenia's peculiar; she's very independent, very fantastic. She likes to do whatever comes into her head. She's very fascinating ... but I shouldn't be at all surprised if she's absolutely cold; I mean, really never could care for any man at all.'

'I *should* like to see her,' repeated Lord Selsey, his eyes brightening.

'It's most awfully good of you, Uncle, the way you take it. I mean to say, I'm afraid I'm not at all asking your consent, you know, or anything of that sort, as I ought.'

'You're asking my advice, and it's about the only thing most men of my age enjoy giving. Well, really, Cecil, and frankly, I think it's a dismal little story. It would be humbug if I pretended I was sorry about Mrs Raymond's—a—attitude, and I quite see its absolute genuineness But, if you'll excuse my saying so, what price the other girl?'

'What price? No price.'

'*She* likes you,' said Lord Selsey acutely. 'What makes

you think that?'

'Because otherwise you wouldn't be so cool about her. You're a little too frightened of being obvious, Cecil. I was like that, too. But don't give way to it. Hyacinth Verney—what a charming name! ... What would old Cannon say?'

'I don't think he seems particularly keen on *me*,' said Cecil frankly.

'That's odd. Then he must be very ambitious for her, or else be in love with her himself ... probably both.'

'Oh, I say, Uncle Ted! Why, there's Lady Cannon! She's a very handsome, gigantic woman, and they have a daughter of their own, a girl called Ella, at school in Paris. She's pretty, too, only a flapper, you know, with a fair plait and a black bow.'

'I should like to see her; what delightful families you get yourself mixed up with, Cecil! If I were you I should certainly cultivate the Verney girl. I know it's no use telling you to do the contrary, as I should if you weren't in your present frame of mind.'

'I should *very* much like you to meet Eugenia,' said Cecil.

'Yes. How shall we arrange it? A dinner at the Savoy or something?'

'No. Somehow that isn't the kind of thing she'd like,' said Cecil.

'I thought not. But if I suddenly go and call on her, even with you, wouldn't it make it too much of a family affair? And I should be so afraid of having the air of trying to persuade her to give you up. I don't want to make a fool of myself, you know.'

Cecil seemed a little stung, though he smiled.

'If she knew you, perhaps it would make her more interested in me!'

'Do you think she'd come and hear some music here,' said Lord Selsey, 'if I wrote and asked her?'

'Yes, I think she might. There's no nonsense about her—about etiquette and things of that sort, I mean.'

'Then that's settled. You tell her about it, and I'll write. On Thursday afternoon. The two young pianists, George Ranger and Nevil Butt, are coming, and the little girl, the new Russian singer.'

'A juvenile party?' asked Cecil, laughing. 'No, only

two or three people.'

'Two or three hundred, I suppose. Well, I'll get Mrs Raymond to come. Thanks so much.'

They shook hands with more than cordiality. As Cecil went out his uncle said—

'You've been most interesting this morning. But the other girl's the one, you know. Don't neglect her.'

He laughed, for he saw the young man was rather flattered at the notion. Evidently, Mrs Raymond was worth knowing.

CHAPTER VIII

The Peculiarities of Raggett

'Oh, Bruce,' said Edith, as she looked up from a Sale Catalogue, 'I *do* wish you would be an angel and let me have a little cash to go to Naylor and Rope's. There are some marvellous bargains—spring novelties—there, and Archie absolutely *needs* one or two things.'

Bruce frowned and sat down to breakfast, rather heavily.

'I object,' he said as he took his coffee, 'on principle—purely on principle— to spring sales. Women buy a lot of things they don't want, and ruin their husbands under the ridiculous impression they're buying bargains.'

'I won't ruin you, dear. I want to get Archie a coat—and a hat. I only want'—she watched his expression—' a sovereign—or two.' She smiled brightly, and passed him the toast.

His manner softened.

'Well, dear, you know I'm not a rich man, don't you?' 'Yes, dear.'

'But I should much prefer that you should get Archie's things at a first-rate place like Wears and Swells, where we have an account, and send me the bill. Will you do that?'

'Of course I will, if you like; but it'll cost more.'

She had often marvelled at a comparative lavishness about cheques that Bruce combined with a curious loathing to parting from any coin, however small.

'Then that's settled. And now I want to speak to you about Raggett.'

He paused, and then said seriously, 'I've absolutely decided and very nearly made up my mind to have Raggett to dinner tonight at the Savoy.'

'The Savoy?'

'Yes, yes; no doubt this little flat is very comfortable'—he looked round the room with marked disdain—'and cook, thanks to you, isn't half *bad* ... but one can't give *dinners* here! And after all I've said to Raggett—oh, one thing and another—I fancy I've given him the impression of a rather

luxurious home. It won't matter if he calls here in the afternoon some day, but for a man like that, I'd rather—yes—the Savoy. You look as if you objected. Do you?'

'Not at all. It'll be rather fun. But I'm so glad you can afford it. We haven't an *account* there, you know.'

'I propose to make a slight sacrifice for once.... I will engage a table and telephone to Raggett. Women never understand that to do things well, once in a way, is sometimes a—a very good thing,' he finished rather lamely.

'All right. I *am* getting curious to see Raggett!'

'My dear Edith, he's nothing particular to *see*, but he's a man who might be—very useful.'

'Oh, shall you take a private room?'

'I don't think so. Why? You can wear what you wore last night.... You looked quite nice in it, and you can take it from me, once for all'—he got up, looked in the glass, and said—'that *Raggett's all right*. Now, tell cook we're dining out. She might have a holiday tonight. A change may do her good; and I shall hope to find the omelette less leathery tomorrow.'

Edith did not point out that Bruce, after specially ordering breakfast punctually at nine, had come down at half-past ten.

'And now I must go.... The dinner was charming last night. It was only spoilt by that empty-headed fool—what's his name—Reeve, who was obviously making up to Hyacinth. Anyone can see she only endures his attentions from politeness, of course. He knows nothing about anything. I found *that* out when we were smoking after dinner; and one can't get a word out of old Cannon.'

Edith was putting Bruce's writing-table in order when she found an open letter in the blotting-book, glanced at the signature, and saw that it was from Raggett. So she eagerly read it, hoping to get some further light on the mysterious man in whose honour Bruce was prepared to offer so extravagant a festivity.

It was written on a rough sheet of paper, with no address. The handwriting was small, compressed, and very untidy. It ran.—

'DEAR OTTLEY,

'Y'rs to hand. I shall be glad to dine with you, as I have told you several times, and I would accept your invitation with pleasure if I knew when and where the dinner was to be. These two points you have always avoided mentioning.

'Y'rs truly,

J.R. RAGGETT'

It struck Edith that it was quite extraordinary, after so many descriptions from Bruce—some vivid, some sketchy, others subtly suggestive—how little she could imagine Raggett.

Notwithstanding quantities of words, nothing, somehow, had ever come out to throw the least glimmer of light either on his character, personality, or walk of life. Not bad, all right, useful, rather wonderful, but quite ordinary and nothing particular, were some of the phrases she recalled. She had never been told anything about his age, nor his appearance, nor how long Bruce had known him. She had only gathered that he wasn't athletic like Goldthorpe (Bruce's golf companion), and that he wasn't in the Foreign Office, and didn't belong to Bruce's club. Where, how, and when could he be useful?

If she seemed bored when Bruce was enthusiastic about him, he was offended; but if she seemed interested and asked leading questions, he became touchy and cautious, almost jealous. Sometimes she had begun to think that Raggett was a Mrs Harris—that there was no such person. There, evidently, she had been wrong.

At eight o'clock that evening, on arriving at the Savoy, Edith decided not to take off her cloak (on the ground of chilliness, but really because it was smarter and more becoming than her dress). Therefore she waited in the outer room while Bruce, who seemed greatly excited, and had given her various contradictory tips about how to behave to their guest, was taking off his coat. Several other people were waiting there. She saw herself in the glass—a pretty, fair, typically English-looking woman, with neatly- chiselled features, well-arranged *blond-cendré* hair, a tall, slight figure, and a very thin neck. She noticed, among the other people waiting, a shabby-looking man of about thirty-five, who looked so intensely uncomfortable that she pitied him. He had a vague, rough, drab beard, colourless hair, which was very thick in front and very thin at the back, quite indefinite features, an undecided expression, and the most extraordinary clothes she had ever seen. The shirt-front was soft, and was in large bulging pleats. He wore an abnormal-looking big black tie, and the rest of the costume suggested a conjurer who had arrived at a children's party in the country and had forgotten his dress-suit, and borrowed various portions of it from different people staying in the house, who were either taller or shorter than himself. The waistcoat ended too soon, and the coat began too late; the collar reminded one of Gladstone; while the buttonhole of orchids (placed, rather eccentrically, very low down on the coat) completed the general effect of political broadmindedness, combined with acute social anxiety.

He looked several times at Edith with a furtive but undisguised admiration. Then Bruce appeared, held out his hand cordially, and said, 'Ah, Raggett, here you are!'

CHAPTER IX

A Musical Afternoon

Lord Selsey often said he disapproved of the ordinary subdivisions of a house, and, especially as he lived alone, he did not see why one should breakfast in a breakfast-room, dine in a dining-room, draw in a drawing- room, and so on. Nevertheless, he had one special room for music. There was a little platform at the end of it, and no curtains or draperies of any kind to obscure or stifle sound. A frieze of Greek figures playing various instruments ran round the walls, which were perfectly plain so that nothing should distract the eye from the pleasures of the ear; but he was careful to avoid that look of a concert-room given by rows of chairs (suggesting restraint and reserved guinea seats), and the music-room was furnished with comfortable lounges and led into a hall containing small Empire sofas, in which not more than two persons could be seated. Therefore the audience at his entertainments often enjoyed themselves almost as much as the performers, which is rare.

This afternoon there was the usual number of very tall women in large highly-decorated hats, smooth-haired young men in coats that went in at the waist, a very few serious amateurs with longish hair, whose appearance did not quite come up to the standard of the *Tailor and Cutter*, and a small number of wistful professional feminine artists in no collars and pince-nez—in fact, the average fashionable, artistic crowd. The two young geniuses, George Ranger and Nevil Butt, had just given their rather electrifying performance, one playing the compositions of the other, and then both singing Fauré together, and a small band of Green Bulgarians were now playing strenuously a symphony of Richard Strauss, when Cecil and Mrs Raymond appeared together. Lord Selsey received her as if she had been an old friend. When they shook hands they felt at once, after one glance at Cecil and then at each other, that they were more than friends—they were almost accomplices.

By one of those fortunate social accidents that are always occurring in London, Lord Selsey had met Hyacinth and Anne Yeo at a party the day before, had been introduced to them, and invited them to hear Ranger and Butt. Hyacinth, aware she was to meet Mrs Raymond, wore her loveliest clothes and sweetest expression, though she could not keep out of her eyes a certain anxiety, especially when she saw that Cecil greeted her with a slight, cold embarrassment that was very different from his usual

manner. He had not expected to meet Hyacinth, and resolved to avoid the introduction he knew she desired. But no man is a match for a woman in a detail of this sort. In the refreshment-room, where Cecil was pressing coffee on Mrs Raymond, Hyacinth walked in, accompanied by Anne, and stood not very far from him. He came up to her, as Hyacinth saw, at Mrs Raymond's instigation.

'Can I get you anything, Miss Verney? Some tea?'

'Thanks, yes. Isn't that Mrs Raymond? I do wish you would introduce me to her.'

Mrs Raymond came forward. Cecil murmured their names. They shook hands. Mrs Raymond looked at her with such impulsive admiration that she dropped a piece of cake. They spoke a few words about the music, and Cecil moved aside.

Anne called him back, not wishing to see him spared anything.

'You mustn't,' said Cecil, 'on any account miss the next thing. It is the wonderful new singer, don't you know—the little girl, Vera Schakoffsky.'

'Oh, very well,' said Hyacinth. 'I'll go,' and she went on with Anne. But when they had returned to the music-room she said to Anne, 'I left my handkerchief,' and went back to the refreshment-room.

A screen was by the door. Just before she had passed it she heard Mrs Raymond say—

'What an angel! How can you not be at her feet? Go and talk to her at once, or I'll never speak to you again!'

'I just shan't!' said Cecil doggedly. 'You make me simply ridiculous. If you won't be nice to me yourself, you needn't throw me at the head of other people.'

Hyacinth turned back and went to the music-room again.

Some time afterwards Cecil joined her, Mrs Raymond having apparently disappeared. The new tenor was singing an old song. Cecil sat down next to Hyacinth on a little Empire sofa.

'Let me look at the programme,' he said. And as he took it from her he pressed her fingers. She snatched her hand angrily away.

'Pray don't do that,' she said in a contemptuous tone. 'Even to obey Mrs Raymond, you needn't do violence to your feelings!'

'Miss Verney! I beg your pardon! But what *do* you mean?'

'Surely you understand. And don't trouble to come and see me any more.'

He looked at her. Her suave social dexterity had vanished. Her eyes were dark with purely human instinctive jealousy. They looked at each other a moment, then Lord Selsey came up and said—

'I'm afraid my attempt at originality hasn't been quite a success. The concert's not as harmonious as I hoped. Come and have tea, Miss Verney.'

Hyacinth did not speak a word to Anne on their way home, nor did she refer to the afternoon, nor answer any remark of Anne's on the subject till that evening, when Anne came into her room to complain of the electric light and make fun of Lord Selsey's guests. Then she found Hyacinth sobbing, and saying—

'I shall get over it. I shall be all right tomorrow. I'm going to cut him out of my life!'

'He'll soon cut in again,' said Anne.

'Indeed he won't! I'm not going to be played with. Preferring an old Japanese who doesn't even *like* him, and then making a fool of me!'

'If she ran after him, and you begged him to stick to her, it would be the other way,' said Anne.

'What do you mean? Hasn't he any real preference?'

'Yes. He's attached to her, fond of her. She's utterly indifferent about him, so he's piqued. So he thinks that's being in love.'

'Then why does he try to deceive me and flirt with me at all?'

'He doesn't. You really attract him; you're suited to him physically and socially, perhaps mentally too. The suitability is so obvious that he doesn't

like it. It's his feeling for you that he fights against, and especially because he sees you care for him.'

'I was horrid enough to him today! I told him never to call here again.' 'To show

your indifference?'

'I made him understand that I wanted no more of his silly flirtation,' said Hyacinth, still tearful.

'If you *really* made him think that, everything will be all right.' 'Really,

Anne, you're clever. I think I shall take your advice.' Anne gave a queer

laugh.

'I didn't know I'd given any, but I will. Whatever he does now, leave him alone!'

'I should think so! Then why did you tell me the other day to keep on hammering?'

'I was quite right the other day.'

'Didn't I look nicer than Mrs Raymond?'

'That's not the point. You talk as if you were rivals on the same platform. She's on a different plane. But he'll get tired in the end of her indifference and remember *you*,' added Anne sardonically.

'Then he'll find I've forgotten *him*. Oh, why am I so unhappy?'

'You're too emotional, but you'll be happy through that too. Please don't make your eyes red. There are other people in the world. Cecil Reeve—'

'And yet there's something so fascinating about him. He's so unlike anybody else.'

'Bosh!' said Anne. 'He's exactly like thousands of other young men. But it just happens you've taken a fancy to him; that's the only thing that makes him different.'

'I hate him,' said Hyacinth. 'Do you dislike him, Anne?'

'Dislike him?' said Anne, turning out one of the lights. 'No, indeed! I loathe him!'

'But why?'

Anne went to the door.

'Because you're a fool about him,' she said somewhat cryptically.

Hyacinth felt somewhat soothed, and resolved to think no more of Cecil Reeve. She then turned up the light again, took her writing materials, and wrote him three long letters, each of which she tore up. She then wrote once more, saying—

'DEAR MR REEVE,

'I shall be at home today at four. Do come round and see me.'

She put it under her pillow, resolving to send it by a messenger the first thing in the morning, and went to sleep.

But this letter, like the others, was never sent. By the morning light she marvelled at having written it, and threw it into the fire.

CHAPTER X

The Troubles of the Ottleys

'Bruce', said Edith, 'you won't forget we're dining with your people tonight?' 'It's a great nuisance.'

'Oh, Bruce!'

'It's such an infernally long way.' 'It's only to Kensington.'

'West Kensington. It's off the map. I'm not an explorer—I don't pretend to be.' He paused a moment, then went on, 'And it's not only the frightful distance and the expense of getting there, but when I do get there…. Do you consider that my people treat me with proper deference?'

'With proper *what?*' asked Edith.

'Deference. I admit I like deference. I need it—I require it; and at my people's—well, frankly, I don't get it.'

'If you need it,' said Edith, 'I hope you will get it. But remember they are your father and mother.'

'What do you mean by that?'

'Well, I mean they know you very well, of course … and all that.' 'Do you imply…?'

'Oh, no, Bruce dear,' she answered hastily; 'of course I don't. But really I think your people are charming'

'To *you* I know they are,' said he. 'It's all very well for you. They are awfully fond of *you*. You and my mother can talk about Archie and his nurse and housekeeping and fashions, and it's very jolly for you, but where's the fun for a man of the world?'

'Your father—' began Edith.

'My father!' Bruce took a turn round the room. 'I don't mind telling you, Edith, I don't consider my father a man of the world. Why, good heavens! when we are alone together, what do you suppose he talks about? He

complains! Finds fault, if you please! Says I don't work—makes out I'm extravagant! Have *you* ever found me extravagant?'

'No, indeed. I'm sure you've never been extravagant—to *me*.'

'He's not on my level intellectually in any way. I doubt very much if he's capable of understanding me at all. Still, I suppose we might as well go and get it over. My people's dinners are a most awful bore to me.'

'How would you like it,' said Edith gently, 'if some day Archie were to call us my people, and talk about us as you do of yours?'

'Archie!' shouted Bruce. 'Good heavens! Archie!' Bruce held out his arm with a magnificent gesture. 'If Archie ever treats me with any want of proper deference, I shall cut him off with a shilling!'

'Do give me the shilling for him now,' said Edith laughing.

The elder Mrs Ottley was a sweet woman, with a resigned smile and a sense of humour. She had a great admiration for Edith, who was very fond of her. No-one else was there on this occasion. Bruce always complained equally, regarding it as a slight if they were asked alone, and a bore if it was a dinner party. The elder Mr Ottley was considerably older than his wife, and was a handsome, clean-shaven elderly man with a hooked nose and a dry manner. The conversation at dinner consisted of vague attempts on Bruce's part to talk airy generalities, which were always brought back by his father to personalities more or less unflattering to Bruce.

Edith and Mrs Ottley, fearing an explosion, which happened rather frequently when Bruce and his father were together, combined their united energy to ward it off.

'And what do you intend the boy to be when he grows up?' asked old Mr Ottley. 'Are you going to make him a useful member of society, or a Foreign Office clerk?'

'I intend my son,' said Bruce—'(a little port, please. Thanks.)—I intend my son to be a Man of the World.'

His father gave a slight snort.

'Be very careful,' said Mrs Ottley to Edith, 'not to let the darling catch cold in his perambulator this weather. Spring is so treacherous!'

'Does he seem to show any particular bent for anything? I suppose hardly—yet?'

'Well, he's very fond of soldiers,' said Edith.

'Ah!' said Mr Ottley approvingly; 'what we want for empire-building is conscription. Every fellow ought to be a soldier some time in his life. It makes men of them '—he glanced round rather contemptuously—'it teaches them discipline.'

'I don't mean,' said Edith hastily, 'that he wants to *be* a soldier. But he likes playing with them. He takes them to bed with him. It is as much as I can do to keep him from eating them.'

'The angel!' said Mrs Ottley.

'You must be careful about that, Edith,' said Bruce solemnly. 'I understand red paint is poisonous.'

'It won't hurt him,' said old Mr Ottley, purely from a spirit of contradiction.

'But he's just as fond of animals,' said Edith quickly, to avert a storm. 'That Noah's Ark you gave him is his greatest pleasure. He's always putting the animals in and taking them out again.'

'Oh, the clever darling!' cried Mrs Ottley. 'You'd hardly believe it, Edith, but Bruce was like that when he was a little boy too. He used to—'

'Oh mother, do shut up!' said Bruce shame-facedly.

'Well, he was very clever,' said Mrs Ottley defiantly. 'You'd hardly think so now perhaps, but the things that child used to say!'

'Don't spoil Archie as his mother spoilt Bruce,' said Mr. Ottley. 'Have you seen the new play at His Majesty's?' asked Bruce.

'No, I haven't. I went to the theatre *last* year,' said old Mr Ottley. '*I* haven't heaps of money to spend on superfluous amusements.'

'Bruce, you're not eating anything,' said Mrs Ottley anxiously. 'Do try some of these almonds and raisins. They're so good! I always get almonds and raisins at Harrod's now.'

Edith seemed much interested, and warmly assented to the simple proposition that they were the best almonds and raisins in the world.

The ladies retired.

'Most trying Mr Ottley's been lately,' said Mrs Ottley. 'Extremely worrying. Do you suppose I have had a single instant to go and order a new bonnet? Not a second! Has Bruce been tiresome at all?'

'Oh, no, he doesn't mean to be,' said Edith.

Mrs Ottley pressed her hand. 'Darling I *know* what it is. What a sweet dress! You have the most perfect taste. I don't care what people say, those Empire dresses are most trying. I think you're so right not to give in to it as so many young women are doing. Fashion indeed! Hiding your waist under a bushel instead of being humbly thankful that you've got one! Archie is the sweetest darling. I see very little likeness to Bruce, or his father. I think he takes after *my* family, with a great look of you, dear. Most unfortunately, his father thinks Bruce is a little selfish … too fond of pleasure. But he's a great deal at home, isn't he, dear?'

'Yes, indeed,' said Edith, with a slight sigh. 'I think it's only that he's always been a little bit spoilt. No wonder, the only son! But he's a great dear, really.'

His mother shook her head. 'Dear loyal girl! I used to be like that too. May I give you a slight hint? Never contradict. Never oppose him. Agree with him, then he'll change his mind; or if he doesn't, say you'll do as he wishes, and act afterwards in the matter as your own judgement dictates. He'll never find it out. What's that?'

A door banged, hasty steps were heard. Bruce came into the drawing-room alone, looking slightly flushed and agitated.

'Where's your father?' asked Mrs Ottley.

'Gone to his study…. We'd better be getting home, Edith.'

Edith and Mrs Ottley exchanged glances. They had not been able to prevent the explosion after all.

CHAPTER XI

At the National Gallery

It was with considerable difficulty and self-restraint that Cecil succeeded in waiting till the next day to see Mrs Raymond after his uncle's party. He was of an age and of a temperament that made his love affairs seem to him supremely urgent and of more importance than anything else in his life.

He called on Mrs Raymond at eleven in the morning on the pretext of having something important to tell her. He found her sitting at her writing-table in a kind of red kimono. Her hair was brushed straight off her forehead, her eyes were sly and bright, and she looked more Japanese than ever.

Cecil told her what Hyacinth had said to him.

'Now, you see, I *can't* go on making up to her any more. She doesn't care a straw about me, and she sees through it, of course. I've done what you asked me. Won't you be nice to me now?'

'Certainly not! She's quite devoted to you. Telling you not to go and see her again! I never heard of anything so encouraging in my life. Now, Cecil,' she spoke seriously, 'that girl is a rare treasure. It's not only that she's a perfect beauty, but I read her soul yesterday. She has a beautiful nature, and she's in love with you. You don't appreciate her. If you take what she said literally, you're much stupider than I gave you credit for being. I—I simply shan't see you again till you've made it up. When you know her better you *must* care for her. Besides, I insist upon it. If you don't—well, you'll have to turn your attention somewhere else. For I seriously mean it. I won't see you.'

He looked obstinate.

'It's a fad of yours, Eugenia.'

'It's not a fad of mine. It's an opportunity of yours—one that you're throwing away in the most foolish way, that you might regret all your life. At any rate, *I'm* not going to be the cause of giving that poor darling another moment's annoyance or uneasiness. The idea of the angelic creature being worried about me! Why, it's preposterous! I'm sure she heard what I said to you when she came in behind the screen. I can't bear it, and I won't have it. Now go and see her, and you're not to come back till you have. I mean it.'

'I don't suppose for a moment—'

'Rubbish! A woman knows. She went home and cried; I know she did, and she's counting the minutes till you see her again. Now, I've lots to do, and you're frightfully in the way. Good-bye.' She held out her hand.

He rose.

'You send me away definitely?'

'Definitely, Your liking for me is pure perverseness.' 'It's pure adoration,' said Cecil.

'I don't think so. It's imagination. However, whatever it is I don't want it.' 'Good-bye, then,' said Cecil.

He went to the door.

'You can let me know when you've seen her.' 'I don't suppose she'll see me.'

'Yes, she will now. It's the psychological moment.'

'You shan't be bothered with me any more, anyhow,' said Cecil in a low voice.

'Good. And do what I tell you.'

He shut the shabby door of the little house with a loud bang, and went out with a great longing to do something vaguely desperate.

Lunch produced a different mood. He said to himself that he wouldn't think of Mrs Raymond any more, and went to call on Hyacinth.

The servant told him she was out.

He was just turning away when Anne Yeo came out. She glanced at him with malicious satisfaction.

'Hyacinth's gone to the National Gallery,' she volunteered. 'Did you want to see her? You will find her there.'

Cecil walked a few steps with her.

'I'm going to the greengrocer's,' continued Anne, 'to complain.' She held a little book in her hand, and he noticed that she wore a golf cap, thick boots, and a mackintosh, although it was a beautiful day.

'I always dress like this,' she said, 'when I'm going to complain of prices. Isn't it a glorious day? The sort of day when everyone feels happy and hopeful.'

'I don't feel either,' said Cecil candidly.

'No, you don't look it. Why not go and see some pictures?' He smiled.

They parted at the corner.

Then Cecil, without leaving any message for Hyacinth, jumped into a hansom, giving the man the address of his club in Pall Mall. On the way he changed his mind, and drove to the National Gallery. As he went up the steps his spirits rose. He thought he recognised Miss Verney's motor waiting outside. There was something of an adventure in following her here. He would pretend it was an accident, and not let her know yet that he had called.

He wandered through the rooms, which were very empty, and came upon Hyacinth seated on a red velvet seat opposite a Botticelli.

She looked more dejected than he could have thought possible, her type being specially formed to express the joy of life. It was impossible to help feeling a thrill of flattered vanity when he saw the sudden change in her expression and her deep blush when she recognised him.

'I didn't know you ever came here,' she said, as they shook hands.

'It's a curious coincidence I should meet you when, for once in my life, I come to study the Primitives,' said Cecil.

He then seated himself beside her.

'Don't you think all that '—he waved his hand towards the pictures—'is rather a superstition?'

'Perhaps; but it's glorious, I think. These are the only pictures that give me perfect satisfaction. All others, however good they are, have the effect of making me restless,' said Hyacinth.

'I haven't had a moment's rest,' said Cecil, 'since I saw you yesterday afternoon. Why were you so unkind?'

'Was it unkind?' she asked. Her face was illuminated.

They spent an hour together; had horrible tea in the dismal refreshment-room, and having agreed that it seemed a shame to spend a lovely day within these walls, he said—

'I don't think I've ever met you out of doors—in the open air, I mean.' 'It would

be nice,' said Hyacinth.

He proposed that they should do something unconventional and delightful, and meet the next day in Kensington Gardens, which he assured her was just as good as the country just now. She agreed, and they made an appointment.

'How is Mrs Raymond?' she then asked abruptly.

'I don't know. Mrs Raymond—she's charming, and a great friend of mine, of course; but we've quarrelled. At least I'm not going to see her again.'

'Poor Mrs Raymond!' exclaimed Hyacinth. 'Or perhaps I ought to be sorry for you?'

'No, not if you let me sec you sometimes.' He looked at her radiant face and felt the soothing, rather intoxicating, effect of her admiration after Eugenia's coldness.... He took her hand and held it for a minute, and then they parted with the prospect of meeting the next day.

Hyacinth went home too happy even to speak to Anne about it. She was filled with hope. He *must* care for her.

And Cecil felt as if he were a strange, newly-invented kind of criminal. Either, he said to himself, he was playing with the feelings of this dear, beautiful creature, or he was drifting into a *mariage de convenance*, a vulgar and mercenary speculation, while all the time he was madly devoted to someone else. He felt guilty, anxious, and furious with Eugenia. But she had really meant what she said that morning; she wouldn't see him again. But the thought of seeing Hyacinth under the trees the next morning—a secret appointment, too!—was certainly consoling.

With a sudden sensation of being utterly sick of himself and his feelings, tired of both Hyacinth and Eugenia, and bored to death at the idea of all women, Cecil went to see Lord Selsey.

CHAPTER XII

More of the Little Ottleys 'Fancy!'

said Edith. 'Fancy what?'

'Somehow I never should have thought it,' said Edith thoughtfully.

'Never should have thought what? You have a way of assuming I know the end of your story before I've heard the beginning. It's an annoying method,' said Bruce.

'I shouldn't have been so surprised if they had been anywhere else. But just *there*,' continued Edith.

'Who? and where?'

'Perhaps I'd better not tell you,' Edith said.

They had just finished dinner, and she got up as if to ring the bell for coffee.

He stopped her.

'No! Don't ring; I don't wish Bennett to be present at a painful scene.'

Edith looked at him. 'I didn't know there was going to be a painful scene. What's the matter?'

'Naturally, I'm distressed and hurt at your conduct.' 'Conduct!'

'Don't echo my words, Edith.'

She saw he looked really distressed.

'Naturally,' he continued, 'I'm hurt at your keeping things from me. Your own husband! I may have my faults—'

She nodded.

'But I've not deserved this from you.'

'Oh dear, Bruce, I was only thinking. I'm sorry if I was irritating. I will tell you.'

'Go on.'

'When Nurse and Archie were out in the Gardens this morning, who do you think they met?'

'This is not a game. I'm not going to guess. You seem to take me for a child.'

'Well, you won't tell anybody, will you?'

'That depends. I'm not going to make any promises beforehand. I shall act on my own judgement.'

'Oh, you might promise. Well, I'll trust you.' 'Thanks! I should think so!'

'They met Hyacinth, walking with Cecil Reeve alone in a quiet part of the Gardens. They weren't walking.'

'Then why did you say they were?' asked Bruce severely. 'It's the same thing. They were sitting down.'

'How *can* it be the same thing?'

'Oh, don't worry, Bruce! They were sitting down under a tree and Nurse saw them holding hands.'

Bruce looked horrified.

'Holding hands,' continued Edith; 'and I can't help thinking they must be engaged. Isn't it extraordinary Hyacinth hasn't told me? What do you think?'

Bruce got up from the table, lighted a cigarette, and walked round the little room.

'I don't know. I must consider. I must think it over.' He paused a minute. 'I am pained. Pained and surprised. A girl like Hyacinth, a friend of yours, behaving like a housemaid out with a soldier in the open street!'

'It wasn't the street, Bruce.' 'It's the same idea.'

'Quite a quiet part of the Gardens.'

'That makes their conduct worse. I scarcely think, after what you have told me, that I can allow you to go out with Hyacinth tomorrow.'

'How can you be so absurd? I must go; I want to hear about it.'

'Have I ever made any objection till now at your great intimacy with Hyacinth Verney? Of course not. Because I was deceived in her.'

'Deceived?'

'Don't repeat my words, Edith. I won't have it! Certainly I was deceived. I thought she was a fitting companion for you—I *thought* so.'

'Oh, Bruce, really! Where's the harm? Perhaps they're engaged; and if they are I think it is charming. Cecil is such a nice, amusing, good-looking boy, and—'

'I formed my opinion of Reeve some time ago.' 'You only

met him once.'

'Once is more than enough for me to form a judgement of anyone. He is absolutely unworthy of her. But her conduct I regard as infinitely worse. I always imagined she was respectably brought up—a lady!'

'Good gracious! Anyone can see that! She's the most charming girl in the world.'

'*Outwardly*, no doubt, she seems all right. But now you see what she is.'

He paused to relight his cigarette, which had gone out, and continued: 'Such behaviour would be dreadful enough in private, but in public! Do you think of the example?'

'The example to Archie, do you mean?'

'Don't laugh, Edith. This is no matter for laughing. Certainly to Archie—to anyone. Now I've only one thing to say.'

'Do say it.'

'That I never wish to hear Hyacinth Verney's name mentioned again. You are never to speak of her to me. Do you hear?'

'Yes, Bruce.'

'It is such a disillusion. I'm so shocked, so horrified, finding her a snake in the grass.'

'Oh, I'm sure she didn't look a bit like a snake, Bruce. She wore that lovely grey dress and a hat with roses.'

'How do you know? Did *Archie* tell you? No; you lowered yourself to question Nurse. A nice opinion Nurse must have of your friends now! No; *that's* over. I won't blame *you*, dear, but I must never hear anything more about Hyacinth.'

Edith sat down and took up a book.

'Why is there no coffee?' asked Bruce rather loudly. 'Oh, you

said I wasn't to ring.'

She rang.

While the parlourmaid was bringing in the coffee, Bruce said in a high, condescending voice—

'Have you seen that interesting article in the evening paper, dear, about the Solicitor-General?'

'Which do you mean? "Silk and Stuff"?'

'Yes. Read it—read it and improve your mind. Far better for a woman to occupy her mind with general subjects, and make herself intellectually a companion for her husband—are you listening?—than to be always gossiping and thinking about people and their paltry private affairs. Do you hear?'

'Yes, dear.'

He took his coffee and then said—

'In what direction did you say they were going?'

'Oh, I thought you didn't want me to speak of her again. They were going in the opposite direction.'

'Opposite to what? Now that's the curious difference between a woman's intellect and a man's. You can't be logical! What do you mean by "opposite"?'.

'Why, Bruce, I mean just opposite. The other way.' 'Do you mean

they walked off separately?'

'Oh, no! They were going away together, and looking so happy. But really, Bruce, I'm sorry I bothered you, telling you about it. I had no idea you would feel it so much.'

'What do you mean? Feel it? Of course, I'm terribly distressed to find that a wife of mine is intimate with such people—where are you going?'

'I was going to write to Hyacinth and tell her I can't go out with her tomorrow.'

'Why can't you go out with her?'

'You said I was never to see her again.'

'Yes; but don't be in a hurry. Never be impulsive.' He waited a minute; she stood by the door. 'On the whole, since you wish it so much, I will permit you to go out with her this once—for the last time, of course—so that you can find out if she really is engaged to be married to that young ass. What a mercenary scoundrel he must be!'

'I don't think that. Anyone would admire her, and he is very well off himself.'

'Well off! Do you consider that to his credit. So should I be well off if I had relations that died and left me a lot of money. Don't defend him, Edith; his conduct is simply disgraceful. What right has he to expect to marry a beautiful girl in Hyacinth's position? Good gracious, does he want everything?'

'I suppose—he likes her.'

'That's not particularly clever of him. So would any man. What I object to so much about that empty-headed cad, is that he's never satisfied. He wants the earth, it seems to me!'

'Really, Bruce, one would think you were quite—' 'What?'

'Well, quite jealous of him, to hear you talk. If one didn't know that—of course you can't be,' she added quickly.

'This incident is now closed,' said Bruce. 'We will never discuss the subject again.'

'Very well, dear.'

She then went into the little drawing-room and looked longingly at the telephone. She feared there would be no chance of communicating with her friend that evening.

Five minutes later Bruce came in and said—

'And what can old Cannon be about to allow his ward to be tearing about all over London with a man of Reeve's antecedents?'

'What's the matter with his antecedents? I didn't know he had any.'

'Don't interrupt. And Miss Yeo? Where was Miss Yeo, I should like to know?'

'I can't *think*.'

'A nice way she does her duty as chaperone!'

'Dear, Hyacinth's twenty-three, not a child. Miss Yeo's her companion; but she can't insist, even if she wants to, on following Hyacinth about if she doesn't wish it.'

'She should wish it. Seriously, do you think Sir Charles knows of these goings-on—I mean of this conduct?'

'I shouldn't think he knew the details.'

'Then isn't it my duty as a married man and father of a family—' Edith

concealed a smile by moving the screen.

'To communicate with him on the subject?'

Edith had a moment's terror. It struck her that if she opposed him, Bruce was capable of doing it. He often wrote letters beginning, 'Sir, I feel it my duty,' to people on subjects that were no earthly concern of his. If he really did anything of this sort, Hyacinth would never forgive her.

After a second's concentration of mind, she said mildly—

'Perhaps you had better, if you really feel it your duty. Of course, I'd rather you didn't, personally. But if that's how you feel about it—'

Bruce wheeled round at once.

'Indeed! Well, I shall not do anything of the sort. Is it my business to open her guardian's eyes? Why should I? No; I won't interfere in the matter at

all. Let them go their own way. Do you hear, Edith? Let them do just whatever they like.'

'Yes; I was going to.'

'Mind you, they'll be wretched,' he added rather vindictively. 'If I only saw a chance of happiness for them I shouldn't mind so much.'

'Why do you think they will be miserable if they are married?'

'Of course they will. People who behave in that unprincipled way before—' 'Why, we

used to sit in the garden,' said Edith timidly.

'Oh, yes, of course; after your father had given his consent.' 'And once

or twice before.'

Bruce smiled rather fatuously. 'Don't compare the two cases. I was a man of the world.... I was very firm, wasn't I Edith? Somehow at first your father didn't seem to like me, but I reasoned with him. I always reason calmly with people. And then he came round. Do you remember how pleased you were that day?' He patted Edith's hair.

'Then why be so severe?'

'Perhaps I am a little bit too severe,' he acknowledged. 'But you don't quite understand how it jars on me to think of any friend of yours behaving in a manner that's—are you sure they're engaged?'

'No; I don't know anything about it.'

'Well, of course, if they don't marry after what Archie has seen, it will be a public scandal, that's all I can say. On the other hand, of course, it would be far better not.'

'What do you propose?' said Edith.

'I don't quite know; I'll think it over. Look here, Edith, if you don't mind, I think I'll go for a little stroll. The flat seems so hot and airless tonight'

Edith glanced at the telephone. 'Oh, don't go,' she said.

He went into the hall and put on his coat. 'I must go, dear. I feel the need of air. I shan't be long.'

'You will only go for a little walk, won't you?'

'I might go to the club for half an hour. I shall see. Good night, dear.' 'Good night.'

He came back to say, in a rather mysterious voice— 'What were Nurse's exact words?'

'Oh, she said, "Miss Verney seemed to be carrying on anyhow with a young gentleman in Kensington Gardens," and then she said it was Mr Reeve, that's all.'

'Disgusting! Horrible!'

He went out and banged the door. Edith went to the telephone.

CHAPTER XIII

Lady Cannon's Visit

Lady Cannon got up one morning earlier than usual and tried on a dress of last season, which she found was a little too tight. For this, naturally, she blamed her maid with some severity. She then dressed rather hurriedly and went all over the house, touching little ornaments with the tip of her finger, saying that the pictures in the drawing-room were crooked, and that nothing had been properly dusted. Having sent for the housemaid and scolded her, and given the second footman notice, she felt better, but was still sufficiently in what is expressively called a bad temper to feel an inclination to do disagreeable duties, so she made up her mind to call and see her husband's ward, and tell her something she would not like to hear. For Hyacinth she always felt a curious mixture of chronic anger, family pride, and admiring disapproval, which combination she had never yet discovered to be a common form of vague jealousy.

Lady Cannon arrived about three o'clock, pompously dressed in tight purple velvet and furs. She thought she saw two heads appear at the studio window and then vanish, but was told that Miss Verney was out.

Prompted by a determination not to be baffled, she said she would get out and write a note, and was shown to the drawing-room.

Anne, in a peculiarly hideous and unnecessary apron of black alpaca, came in, bringing a little writing-case.

'Oh! Miss Yeo, as you're there, I needn't write the letter. You can give Hyacinth a message for me.'

'Certainly, Lady Cannon.'

'How is it that she is out at this extraordinary hour?'

'Is there anything extraordinary about the hour?' asked Anne, looking at the clock. 'It's three; somehow I always regard three as a particularly ordinary hour.'

'I differ from you, Miss Yeo.'

'Anyhow, it happens every day,' murmured Anne.

'Was Hyacinth out to lunch?' said Lady Cannon. 'No—no.

She lunched at home.'

'Do you think she'll be long?'

'Oh, no; I shouldn't think she would be many minutes.' 'Then I

think I'll wait.'

'*Do*,' said Anne cordially.

'I wanted to speak to her. Considering she's my husband's ward, I see very, very little of Hyacinth, Miss Yeo.'

'Yes, she was saying the other day that you hardly ever called now,' Anne said conciliatingly.

'Has she been quite well lately?'

'Oh, do you know, she's been so well,' said Anne, in a high, affected voice, which she knew was intensely irritating. 'So very, very well!'

Anne then stood up.

'Would you like a cup of tea, or coffee, while you're waiting?'

'*Tea*? At three o'clock in the afternoon! I never heard of such a thing. You seem to have strangely Bohemian ideas in this house, Miss Yeo!'

'Do you think tea Bohemian? Well, coffee then?'

Lady Cannon hesitated, but wishing for an excuse to wait, she said—

'Thank you, if it isn't giving any trouble; perhaps I'll take a cup of coffee. I didn't have any after lunch.'

'Oh, yes, do. I'll go and order it at once.'

Anne walked with slow, languid dignity to the door, and when she had shut it, flew like a hunted hare to the studio, where Cecil Reeve and Hyacinth were sitting together.

'Hyacinth,' she said sharply, 'run upstairs at once, put on your hat, go to the hall door and bang it, and come into the drawing-room. Lady Cannon's going to stop the whole afternoon. She's in an appalling temper.'

'She won't wait long,' exclaimed Hyacinth, 'surely?'

'Won't she? She's ordered coffee. She'll be smoking a cigarette before you know where you are.'

'Oh, I'll go,' said Cecil. 'Let me go.'

'Of course you must go,' said Anne. 'You can come back in an hour.'

'But, good heavens, Anne,' said Hyacinth, 'why on earth should we make a secret of Mr Reeve being here?'

'Why, because I said you were out.' 'Well, I'll go

and explain,' said Hyacinth.

'Indeed you won't. You're not to go and give me away. Besides, I won't be baffled by that old cat. She's suspicious already. Out you go!'

Cecil took his hat and stick, and went out of the front door.

Anne ran upstairs, brought down Hyacinth's hat, veil, and gloves, and pushed her towards the drawing-room.

'Don't you see?—she'll think you've just come in,' said Anne. 'What

about the coachman and footman?'

'Oh, good heavens, do you think they're going to call on her and tell her all about it?'

Just as Hyacinth, laughing, was going into the drawing-room, Anne clutched her, and said—

'I don't know that you'd better be at home after all! Charles will be calling directly. Oh, I forgot, he won't come in when he sees the carriage.'

Anne relaxed her clasp and went to order coffee.

Lady Cannon was looking angrily in the glass when Hyacinth came in.

'Oh, here you are, my dear. I'm glad I didn't miss you. I wanted to speak to you about something.'

'Yes, Auntie.'

Lady Cannon coughed, and said rather portentously, 'You must not be offended with me, dear. You know, in a sense I'm, as it were, in the place of your mother—or, at any rate, your stepmother.'

'Yes.'

'Of course you're perfectly free to do exactly as you like, but I heard in a roundabout way something that rather surprised me about you.'

'What is it?'

'We were dining with some friends last night' (it was characteristic of Lady Cannon not to mention their names), 'where we happened to meet that young couple, the Ottleys. You know Mrs Ottley very well, I believe?'

'Edith is my greatest friend,' said Hyacinth.

'Quite so; she seems a very nice young woman. Very devoted to her husband. And I think him a most superior man! He sat next to me at dinner, and I had quite a long talk with him. We spoke of you. He told me something that surprised me so much. He said that you had been seen very frequently lately about alone with a young man. Is this a fact?'

'What did he say about it?'

'Well, he seemed to regret it—he seemed to think it was a pity. Living alone as you do, it certainly is not the right thing for you to be seen anywhere without Miss Yeo.'

Hyacinth became crimson. 'On what grounds did Mr Ottley find fault with anything I do?'

'Merely general grounds, my dear. A very proper dislike to the flighty behaviour of the girls of the present day. As he tells me, he feels it as a father—'

'Father! He has only a little boy of two. I think it's very impertinent of him to talk of me like that at all.'

'On the contrary, I thought it exceedingly nice of him. He sincerely wishes you well, Hyacinth. Oh, *how* well that young man wishes you! Make no mistake about it. By the way, I promised him not to mention his name in the matter. So of course you won't repeat it. But I was really rather upset at what he said. I haven't said anything to Sir Charles yet, as I thought you might give me some explanation.'

'I have no explanation to give. I suppose you know who it is I was walking with?'

'I gathered that it was a Mr Reeve. Now, Hyacinth dear, you know how much I wish you well; if you're engaged, I think your guardian and I ought

to know it, and in any case you should be more discreet in your behaviour.'

Hyacinth's eyes flashed.

'Are you engaged?' asked Lady Cannon.

'I must decline to answer. I recognise no right that you or anyone else has to ask me such a question.'

Lady Cannon rose indignantly, leaving her coffee untouched.

'Very well, Hyacinth; if this is the way you take my kind advice and well-meant interest, there's nothing more to be said. Of course, I shall tell Sir Charles what I've heard. From what I can gather from that excellent young man Mr Ottley, Mr Reeve is by no means a person that Sir Charles and I would be glad to welcome with open arms, as one of the family.'

'Cecil Reeve is a friend of mine. There's nothing in the world to be said against him, and you must really allow me the privilege of choosing my own friends.'

'Good-bye then,' said Lady Cannon, going to the door. 'I'm pained, grieved, and shocked at your attitude. I can only presume, however, that you are not engaged to be married, for surely your first thought would have been to ask your guardian's consent; and once more let me tell you, in being reckless as you have, you're simply ruining your future.'

With this Lady Cannon swept from the room.

She returned, however, and said, 'I regard all this as not your own fault, Hyacinth, but the fault of *that Miss Yeo*. From the first I saw she had an evil influence, and I've been proved, as, perhaps unfortunately, I always am, to be perfectly right.'

'The worst of it was,' Hyacinth said, when relating the conversation to Anne a little later,' that I *can't* tell Auntie that I'm engaged. Isn't it awful?'

'You soon will be,' said Anne consolingly. 'Do you really

think so?'

'Yes, and I'm glad Lady Cannon was scored off, anyhow.'

'Edith told me about her having mentioned to Bruce about our meeting the nurse and baby. She was very sorry, but I thought it didn't matter a bit. Why do you think Bruce tried to make mischief in this horrid way?'

'Only because he's a fool. Like so many of us, he's in love with you,' said Anne.

Hyacinth laughed, thinking Anne was in fun.

CHAPTER XIV

Raggett in Love

'If you please, ma'am a gentleman called and left some flowers.' 'Who was it?' said Edith.

'He wouldn't give his name. There's a note for you.'

Edith went into the drawing-room, where she found a large bundle of lilies, violets, and daffodils, and the following letter, written in a cramped, untidy handwriting:—

'DEAR MRS OTTLEY,

'I went for a bicycle ride yesterday and plucked these flowers for you, hoping you wouldn't mind accepting them. If you have a moment's time to give me, I wonder if you would let me call and see you one day?

'Sincerely yours,

'F. J. RAGGETT

'P.S.—I'm extremely busy, but am free at any time. Perhaps tomorrow might suit you? Or if you're engaged tomorrow, perhaps today? I would ask you to ring me up and kindly let me know, but I'm not on the telephone.'

Edith was amused, but also a little bored. Ever since the dinner at the Savoy, now a fortnight ago, Raggett had been showing furtive signs of a wild admiration for her, at the same time hedging absurdly by asking her to tell him when he might call and giving no address, and by (for instance) pretending he had plucked the flowers himself, evidently not knowing that they had been sent with her address written on a card printed with the name of Cooper's Stores in the Edgware Road.

She never knew how Bruce would take things, so she had not said anything about it to him yet. He seemed to have forgotten the existence of Raggett, and never mentioned him now.

She arranged the flowers in some blue and white china vases, and sat down by the window in the little drawing-room. She had before her, until Bruce would come home to dinner, two of those empty hours which all young married women in her position have known. There was nothing to

do. Archie was still out, and she was tired of reading, and disliked needlework.

She had just come back from seeing Hyacinth. How full and interesting *her* life seemed! At any rate, *she* had everything before her. Edith felt as if she herself were locked up in a box. Even her endless patience with Bruce was beginning to pall a little.

As she was thinking these things she heard a ring, and the maid came in and said—

'It's the gentleman that left the flowers, and could you see him for a minute?'

'Certainly.'

Raggett came in. He looked just as extraordinary as he had at the Savoy and as difficult to place. His manner could not be said to express anything, for he had no manner, but his voice was the voice of a shy undergraduate, while his clothes, Edith thought, suggested a combination of a bushranger and a conjuror. His tie, evidently new, was a marvel, a sort of true-lover's knot of red patterned with green, strange beyond description. He seemed terrified.

'How very kind of you to come and see me,' she said in her sweetest voice, 'and these lovely flowers! They quite brighten one up.'

'I'm glad you think they're all right,' said Raggett in a low voice.

'They're beautiful. Fancy your plucking them all yourself! Where did you find these lovely lilies growing? I always fancied they were hot-house plants.'

'Oh, I was bicycling,' Raggett said. 'I just saw them, you know. I thought you might like them. How is Ottley?'

'Bruce is very well. Haven't you seen him lately?'

'Not very. I've been working so fearfully hard,' he said; 'at the British Museum chiefly. One doesn't run up against Bruce there much.'

'No. I suppose he hardly ever goes.' There was a pause.

'Won't you have some tea?' asked Edith.

'No, thank you. I never take it.' And there was another silence.

Just as Edith was rather at a loss, and was beginning a sentence with— 'Have you been—' he at the same time said—

'Do you know—?'

'I beg your pardon,' said Edith. 'Oh, I beg yours.'

'Do say what you were going to say.' 'Oh, please finish your sentence.'

'I wasn't going to say anything.' 'Nor was I.'

'I was going to ask you if you'd been to the Savoy again lately?'

'No; I've only been there once in my life. It was a great event for me, Mrs Ottley.'

'Really?'

He spoke with more confidence, but in a still lower voice. 'Yes. I met my ideal there.'

He fixed on her an ardent but respectful glare. She smiled.

'I'm afraid,' continued Raggett, 'that I'm not amusing you much. I suppose you're very fond of wit and gaiety? I wasn't brought up in a very humorous atmosphere. I don't think I ever heard a joke till quite recently.'

Edith laughed.

'My father,' he went on, 'used sometimes to say at night. "Now it's time for Bedfordshire," but I wasn't amused at that after ten years old. My family are really very serious as a whole. I should never dream of asking them even a riddle, because I'm sure they would give it up at once.'

'Did you say you heard one joke recently? What was it?' asked Edith.

Raggett blushed and looked down.

'I'm very sorry, but I'm afraid I can't tell you, Mrs Ottley. Not that I forget it, but it isn't suited to your—well, to your atmosphere'—he looked round the room.

'Oh! Can't you *arrange* it?'

'Impossible,' he said firmly. 'Quite impossible.' 'Oh well, of course—'

'Impossible,' he repeated, shaking his head.

'Do you go much to the theatre?' she asked conversationally. 'Never. It would interfere with my work.'

'What is your work, exactly?' she asked, with polite interest. 'It's difficult to explain, Mrs Ottley. It takes a great many forms.' 'Oh, yes.'

'Just at this moment I'm a Legitimist—you understand, don't you? We drink to Queen Mary over the water—and put violets on the statue of King Charles the Martyr in February, and so forth.'

'Ah. That must be very hard work.'

'Oh, it isn't only that—I'm a kind of Secretary, you see, to the Society.'

'Really? Really? What fun it must be; I mean how interesting. Can I belong?'

'Oh, dear yes, of course, Mrs Ottley. If you liked.' 'What should I have to do?'

'Well, first of all you would have to pay a shilling.' 'Yes?'

'And then you would be eligible for a year's probation.' 'And what should we do after that?'

'Well, after that, you see, we shall have to bide our time.'

'That doesn't sound very hard,' said Edith thoughtfully. 'Just to pay a shilling and bide your time.'

'I'll send you some papers about it, if you really take any interest.' 'Thanks. Thanks, very much. Yes, do send them.'

'Do you really think you would care to become a member, Mrs Ottley?' 'Oh, yes; yes, I should think so. I always hated Oliver Cromwell.'

He looked doubtful.

'Yes, of course—but that alone, I'm afraid, would hardly be … you see there might be a revolution at any moment.'

'I see. But—excuse my asking you, what has that to do with the British Museum?'

'I can hardly tell you off-hand like this, Mrs Ottley; but if you let me come again one day—'

'Oh, certainly, do—do come again.'

'Then I'll say good-bye for today,' said Raggett, with an admiring look. 'I—I hope I haven't trespassed on your valuable—'

'Oh, no; not in the least.'

'I've enjoyed our talk so much,' said Raggett, lingering. 'So have I, Mr Raggett. It has been most interesting.'

'I—I felt,' said Raggett, now standing up and looking very shy, 'I somehow felt at once that there was a kind of—may I say, sympathy?'

'Quite so.'

'Yes? Well, give my kind regards to Ottley, and thank you so much.'

They shook hands, she rang the bell, and he rushed out as if he was in a violent hurry, leaving Edith rather bewildered.

At dinner that evening Edith said— 'Fancy, Bruce, Raggett called today!'

Bruce dropped his spoon in the soup and looked up.

'*Raggett*? He—do you mean to say he came here?' 'Yes. He paid a visit. Why shouldn't he?'

'I don't know, but it seems a very odd thing. He never pays visits. What did he seem to think of the flat?'

'He didn't say. He talked about his work.' 'What did you think of him?' asked Bruce.

'He seemed very vague. He's very good-natured; fancy his sending me all those flowers!'

'He sent you flowers?' said Bruce slowly. '*Raggett*!' 'Surely you don't mind?'

Bruce waited a minute and said, 'We'll talk it over after dinner.' There was an uneasy pause; then Edith said—

'I saw Hyacinth today. She had just had a visit from Lady Cannon.' Bruce looked rather guilty and uncomfortable.

'I like Lady Cannon,' he said presently. 'She's a woman of sound sense. She has a very strong feeling of responsibility about Hyacinth.'

'Yes.' Edith and Hyacinth had arranged not to say any more, as it would be useless.

'A very discreet woman, too,' continued Bruce. 'And what news about Hyacinth?'

'None, I think. She seems very happy.' 'Happy! *That* can't last.'

After dinner Bruce followed Edith into the drawing-room, looked angrily at the flowers and said—

'Now what's the meaning of all this? Mind, I'm not jealous. It isn't my nature to be. What I dislike is being made a fool of. If I thought that Raggett, after all I've done for him—'

'Oh, Bruce! How can you be so absurd? A poor harmless creature—'

'Harmless creature, indeed! I think it extremely marked, calling on you when I was out.'

'He didn't know you were out. It's the usual time to pay a visit, and he really came just to ask me to belong to the Society.'

'I don't call Raggett a society man.'

'He's a secret-society man,' said Edith. 'He wants me to be a Legitimist.'

'Now I won't have any nonsense of that sort here,' said Bruce, striking the table with his fist. 'Goodness knows where it will end. That sort of thing takes women away from the natural home duties, and I disapprove of it strongly. Why, he'll soon be asking you to be a Suffragette! I think I shall write to Raggett.'

'Oh, would you, really?'

'I shall write to him,' repeated Bruce, 'and tell him that I won't have these constant visits and marked attentions. I shall say you complained to me. Yes, that's the dignified way, and I shall request him to keep his secret societies to himself, and not to try to interfere with the peace and harmony of a happy English home.'

He drew some writing-paper towards him.

'I'm sure he didn't mean the slightest harm. He thought it was the proper thing, after dining with us.'

'But it isn't like the man, Edith! It isn't Raggett! He's no slave to convention; don't think it. I can't help fancying that there must have been some ulterior motive. It seems to me sinister—that's the word—sinister.'

'Would you think it sinister if he never came, again?'

'Well, perhaps not, but in allowing this to pass—isn't it the thin end of the wedge?'

'Give him a chance and see,' she said. 'Don't be in a hurry. After all, he's your great friend. You're always talking to me about him; and what's he done?—sent a few flowers and called here once. I'm sure he thought you would like it.'

'But don't you see, Edith, the attention should have been paid to me, not to you.'

'He could hardly send you flowers, Bruce. I'm sure he thought it was the proper thing.'

Bruce walked up and down the room greatly agitated.

'I admit that this is a matter that requires consideration. I shouldn't like to make a mountain out of a mole-hill. We'll see; we'll give him a chance. But if he comes here again, or takes any step to persuade you to have anything to do with his Society or whatever it is, I shall know how to act.'

'Of course you will, dear.'

Edith hoped she wouldn't receive a large envelope full of papers about the Legitimists by the first post.

'I hope you know, Bruce, *I* shouldn't care if I never saw him again.'

'Why not? Because he's my friend, I suppose? You look down on him just because he's a hard worker, and of some use in the world—not a dandified, conventional, wasp-waisted idiot like Cecil Reeve! Perhaps you prefer Cecil Reeve?'

'Much,' replied Edith firmly. 'Why? Let's

hear your reasons.'

'Why, he's a real person. I know where I am when I'm talking to him— we're on the same platform.'

'Platform?'

'Yes. When I talk to Mr Raggett I feel as if he had arrived at Victoria, and I had gone to meet him at Charing Cross. Do you see? We don't get near enough to understand each other.'

'Quite near enough,' replied Bruce suspiciously. Then he said, 'I feel the want of air. If you don't mind, dear, I think I shall go for a stroll.'

'Oh, don't!'

He went to the hall and put on his coat.

'Just a stroll; or I may look in at the club. You don't understand; a man feels rather cramped in these surroundings, Edith.'

'I quite understand your feeling.'

'I shan't be long,' said Bruce. 'Try and make up your mind to give up Raggett's society altogether. You don't mind making this sacrifice for me, do you?'

'Not in the least,' she answered. 'I prefer it.' He went

out.

CHAPTER XV

Archie

It was Sunday afternoon, and Bruce, lunch still pervading his consciousness, found himself reading over and over again and taking a kind of stupefied interest in the 'Answers to Correspondents' in a certain Sunday paper, and marvelling at the mine of extraordinary miscellaneous information possessed by the person who answered them.

'Brief replies:—

'To *Miserable Alfred* (Baldness).—If you comply with the rules, will send private advice.

'*Knutford* (For knee trouble).—My advice is against.' (Bruce vaguely thought this rather harsh. If Knutford liked knee trouble, why shouldn't he have it?)

'*Alter Ego* (Tomato culture).—There's no need to soak the seeds for days. The man who sows in wet soil and then treads down flat foredooms himself to complete failure. This is, however, nothing to go by. If seed be purchased let it be from a trustworthy firm. Personally, I think in the case of outdoor tomatoes the middle course is best.

'*Worried* (Photography).—To avoid curling. The chief trouble with reel films is their tendency to curl. In any case the film should be allowed to soak for five minutes, and I need not dwell upon other methods of treating the latter kind. All my remarks on plate development, etc., apply equally to cut films, as I should almost have thought 'Worried' would have gathered by now.

'*True Blue* (Egg-preserving).—We quite understand your desire to make more headway than you can in a south-coast watering-place....'

At this moment Edith came in. Bruce looked up a little annoyed at the interruption. He was becoming quite absorbed in the egg-preserving case on the south coast, and morbidly anxious to know what would happen next.

'Bruce, I wonder if you'd do me a very great favour? It really isn't difficult. I've allowed nurse to go out and Bennett is busy, and I wanted to fly over just for a minute or two to see Hyacinth. She telephoned to me. I shouldn't be gone more than twenty minutes.'

'Of course, go. Do go. I don't want you. I'm very busy.' He took up

the paper again.

'It isn't that; but *would* you very much mind looking after Archie while I'm gone? He'll be perfectly good. I'll give him his box of toys, and he'll sit in the corner over there and you'll never notice he's there till I'm back again.'

'Of course, of course. Surely I'm capable of looking after my own son. Do go.'

'Yes, Bruce dear. And if he asks for anything just nod and smile and don't give it to him, and he'll be all right.'

'Oh, don't worry.'

As she was going out he called out—

'And I say, Edith, just give him a hint that I've got some rather important work to do, and he mustn't interrupt me by asking foolish questions.'

'Yes, oh yes. I'm so glad to think you're so sensible, and not ridiculously nervous of having to look after the child.'

'Nervous? What rot! I never heard such nonsense. I say, Edith, what's the doctor's address? In case he has a fit, or anything.'

'Oh, Bruce! As if he would *dream* of having a fit! I shan't give you the address. You'd be telephoning to him on the chance. Good gracious, don't make such a fuss! I shall only be gone a few minutes.'

'I'm not making a fuss. It's you. Fancy thinking it necessary to tell me not to give him what he asks for! As if I should.'

He returned to his paper, and Edith brought in the little boy.

He gave his father a keen glance from under his smooth, fair fringe and sat down in front of the box of toys.

As soon as Edith had gone he held out a card to his father, and said— 'E for

efalunt.'

Bruce frowned, nodded, waved his hand, and went on reading.

He had lost the thread of the Egg Question, but became equally absorbed in the following problem.

'*Disheartened*.—You must make a quiet but determined stand against such imposition. It does not follow because you walked out with a young man two or three times, and he now walks out with your friend instead, that ...'

'X for swordfish,' said Archie, holding out another card. 'Don't talk,

Archie.'

'I've got my best suit on,' said Archie. 'Yes.'

'What I was photographed in.' 'Don't talk, old

chap. I want to read.'

'This is my bear. It's the same bear.' 'The same

bear as what?'

'Why, the same bear! This is a soldier.'

He put the wooden soldier in his mouth, then put it carefully back in the box.

'This is my bear,' said Archie again. 'Just the same bear. That's all.' Bruce

threw away the paper.

'You want to have a talk, eh?' he said.

'This is my best suit,' said Archie. 'Have you any sugar in your pockets?' 'Sugar in my pockets? Who put that into your head?'

'Nobody didn't put it in my head. Don't you put any in your pocket?' 'No. Sugar, indeed! I'm not a parrot.'

Archie roared with laughter.

'You're not a parrot!' he said, laughing loudly. 'Wouldn't it be fun if you was a parrot. I wish you was a parrot.'

'Don't be foolish, Archie.'

'Do parrots keep sugar in their pockets?' 'Don't be silly.'

'Have parrots got pockets?' 'Play with your soldiers, dear.' 'Do parrots have pockets?' 'Don't be a nuisance.'

'Why did you say parrots had sugar in their pockets, then?' 'I never said anything of the kind.'

'What do parrots have pockets for?' 'Do you think your mother will be long?'

'Will mother know about parrots and pockets?'

'You're talking nonsense, Archie. Now be good. Your mother said you would be good.'

'Is it naughty to talk about parrots—with pockets?' 'Yes.'

'Then you're very naughty. You talk about them.'

'Will you stop talking about them if I get you some sugar?' said Bruce, feeling frightfully ashamed of himself, but fearing for his reason if Archie said any more on the subject.

'I'm a good boy. I'll stop talking about parrots if you get me some sugar.' He put his hand in his father's with a most winning smile.

'I'll show you where it is. It's in the kitchen. It's in the nursery, too, but it's nicer sugar in the kitchen.'

'I oughtn't to give it you. Your mother will be angry.' 'Do parrots have pockets?'

Bruce jumped up and went with the child, and told the cook to give him six lumps of sugar.

She seemed surprised, amused, and doubtful. 'Do as I tell you at once,' Bruce said sternly.

They came back, and Archie was silent and happy until Edith returned.

When she saw traces of sugar on his face and dress she said— 'Oh, Archie! What on earth did your father give you sugar for?' 'For talking about parrots,' said Archie.

CHAPTER XVI

Bruce's Play

'Edith,' said Bruce, 'come in here. I want to speak to you. Shut the door.' She shut it, and stood waiting.

'Don't stand there. Come and sit down…. Now listen to me very seriously. I want to ask you a question.'

'How would you like me to be making about £5,000 a year—at least?' 'Need you ask?'

'And all by my own talent—not by anybody else's help.' 'It would be jolly,' she said, trying not to look doubtful.

'Jolly! I should think it would. Now I'll tell you my scheme—what I've made up my mind to do.'

'What?'

'I'm going to write a play.'

Edith controlled her expression, and said it was a very good idea.

'*Such* a play,' said Bruce. 'A really strong, powerful piece—all wit and cynicism like Bernard Shaw—*but*, full of heart and feeling and sentiment, and that sort of rot. It'll have all sorts of jolly fantastic ideas—like *Peter Pan* and *The Beloved Vagabond*, but without the faults of Locke and Barrie—and it's going to be absolutely realistic and natural in parts—like the Sicilians, you know. However, I don't mind telling you that my model— you must have a model, more or less—is going to be Bernard Shaw. I like his style.'

'It's the most lovely idea I ever heard of. What theatre are you going to produce it at?'

'That depends. For some things I should prefer His Majesty's, but I'm rather fond of the Haymarket, too. However, if the terms were better, I might give it to Charlie Hawtrey, or even Alexander, if he offered me exceptionally good royalties.'

'Oh! Are you going to have it put up to auction?'

'Don't talk nonsense. What do you mean? No, I shall simply send a copy round to all the principal people and see what they say.'

He walked up and down the room once or twice.

'The reason I'm so determined not to let Bourchier have it is simply this: he doesn't realise my idea—he never could. Mind you, I believe he would do his best, but his Personality is against him. Do you see, Edith?'

'I see your point. But—'

'There's no reason why it shouldn't be quite as great a success as *The Merry Widow*.'

'Oh, is it going to be a comic opera?'

'Why, of course not. Don't I tell you it's to be a powerful play of real life.' 'Will you

tell me the plot?'

He smiled rather fatuously. 'I'll tell you some of the plot, certainly, if you like—at least, I'll tell you how it's going to begin.'

'Do go on!'—

'Well, I must tell you it begins in a rather unconventional way—entirely different from most plays; but that'll make it all the more striking, and I *won't* alter it—mind that—not for anybody. Well, the curtain goes up, and you find two servants—do you see?—talking over their master and mistress. The maid—her name's Parker—is dusting the photographs and things, and she says to the manservant something about "The mistress does seem in a tantrum, doesn't she, Parker?" So he says—'

'But are they both called Parker?' asked Edith.

'Yes—no—of course not. I forgot; it's the man that's called Parker. But that isn't the point. Well, they talk, and gradually let out a little of the plot. Then two friends of the hero come in, and—oh, I can't bother to tell you any more now; but isn't it rather a good idea, eh? So new!'

'Capital! Splendid! Such a lovely original idea. I do wish you'd be quick and do it, Bruce.'

'I am being quick; but you mustn't be in too great a hurry; you must give me time.'

'Will it be ready in time for the season—I mean after Easter?'

'What! in a fortnight? How could they be ready to produce it in a fortnight, especially with the Easter holidays between? It won't be long, that I can promise you. I'm a quick worker.'

He waited a minute, and then said—

'You mustn't be depressed, Edith dear, if I get a little slating from some of the critics, you know. You can't expect them all to appreciate a new writer at once. And it really won't make any difference to the success if my play pleases the public, which I don't mind telling you I know it's sure to do; because, you see, it'll have all the good points and none of the bad ones of all the successful plays of the last six years. That's my dodge. That's how I do it.'

'I see.'

'Won't it be a joke when the governor and the mater are there on the first night? They'll be frightfully pleased. You must try and prevent the mater swaggering about it too much, you know. She's such a dear, she's sure to be absurdly proud of it. And it'll be a bit of a score off the governor in a way, too. He never would have thought I could do it, would he? And Raggett will be surprised, too. You must have a ripping new dress for the first night, Edith, old girl.'

'I think I shall have Liberty satin, dear—that new shade of blue—it wears better than Nattier. But I won't order it just yet. You haven't written the first scene, have you?'

'The first scene? No! Plays aren't done like that. The chief thing about a play like this is to get a scenario.'

'Oh! Isn't that where the people sit?'

'Don't be ridiculous! You're thinking of the auditorium. I mean the skeleton of the play. That's what I shall send round to the managers. They can see what it's going to be like at once.'

'How many acts will it be?' 'Four.'

'And have you settled on the name?'

'Yes, as a matter of fact I have settled on a name; but don't you go giving it away. It's rather an original name. It would do if I developed the comedy

interest just the same and just as well as if I made the chief point the tragic part. It's going to be called *You Never Know*. Good name, isn't it?'

'It's a splendid name. But isn't it a tiny bit like something else?'

'How unsympathetic you are! The fact is you don't understand. That's what it is.'

'Oh, I do sympathise immensely, Bruce, and I'm sure you'll have a great success. What fun it will be! Are you going to work at it this afternoon?'

'Why, no! not *this* afternoon. I'm rather tired out with thinking. I think I shall go and look in at the club.'

CHAPTER XVII

Hyacinth Waits

'He's coming this afternoon, Anne,' Hyacinth said. 'See that I'm really alone today—I mean that I'm out to everyone.'

'You think, then, that he really will propose today?'

'Don't be so horribly explicit. Don't you think his having to go the other day—because of Lady Cannon—would lead to a sort of crisis? I mean, either he wouldn't come here again, or else—'

'I suppose it would,' said Anne. 'At least, it would if he had some glimmering of his own intentions. But he's in such a very undecided state.'

'Well, don't let's worry about his intentions. At any rate, he's coming to see me. The question is, what shall I wear?'

'It doesn't matter in the least. You attach a ridiculous amount of importance to dress.'

'Perhaps; but I must wear something. So what shall it be?'

'Well, if you want to look prepared for a proposal—so as to give him a sort of hint—you'd better wear your pale mauve dress. It's becoming, and it looks festive and spring-like.'

'Oh, Anne! Why, it's ever so much too smart! It would be quite ridiculous. Just like you, advising pale mauve *crêpe de Chine* and Irish lace for a quiet visit in the afternoon from a friend!'

'Oh! all right. Then wear your blue tailor-made dress—and the little boots with the cloth tops.'

'Oh, good heavens, Anne! I'm not going for a bicycle ride. Because I'm not got up for a garden-party, it doesn't follow I must be dressed for mountain-climbing. Cecil hates sensible-looking clothes.'

'Then I should think anything you've got would do. Or do you want to get a new dress?'

'Of course I want to get a new dress, but not for this afternoon. It wouldn't be possible. Besides, I don't think it's a good plan to wear something different every time you see a person. It looks so extravagant.'

'Wear your black and white, then.'

'No, it isn't *intime* enough, and the material's too rough—it's a hard dress.'

'Oh! Funny, I had the impression you had more clothes than you knew what to do with, and you don't seem to have anything fit to wear.'

'Why, of course, I shall wear my blue voile. How on earth could I wear anything else? How silly you are, Anne!'

'Well, if you knew that all the time, why did you ask me?' 'Are there plenty of flowers in the studio?'

'Yes; but I'll get some more if you like.'

'No, no; don't have too many. It looks too *arranged*.' She looked at the clock.

'It won't be five just yet,' said Anne. 'It's only eleven.'

'Yes; that's the awful part. What on earth shall I do till then?' 'Whatever I suggested you would do the reverse.'

'Shall I go for a long drive in the motor?' 'That's a good idea.'

'But it's a very windy day, and I might get neuralgia—not feel up to the mark.'

'So you might. I think, perhaps, the best thing for you would be to have your hair waved.'

'How can I sit still to have my hair waved? Besides, it makes it look too stiff—like a hairdresser's dummy.'

'Ah! there is that. Then why not do something useful—go and be manicured?'

'I'm afraid I shouldn't have the patience today.'

'I suppose what you'd really like,' said Anne, 'would be to see Edith Ottley.'

'No, I shouldn't. Not till tomorrow. I don't want to see anybody,' said Hyacinth.

'Well, all right. I'm going out.' 'Oh, but I can't bear to be alone.' 'Then I scarcely see …'

'This afternoon especially, Anne. You must stay with me till about a quarter of an hour before I expect him. The horrible agony of waiting is so frightful! It makes me feel so ill. But I don't want you to stay beyond the time I expect him, in case he's late. Because then I suffer so much that I couldn't bear you to see it.'

'I see. How jolly it must be to be in love! You *do* seem to have a good time.'

'When one has the slightest hope, Anne, it's simply too awful. Of course, if one hasn't, one bears it.'

'And if one has no encouragement, I suppose one gets over it?'

'I have a presentiment that everything will be all right today,' said Hyacinth. 'Is that a bad sign?'

'There are no good signs, in your present state,' answered Anne.

It was about half-past four, and Hyacinth in the blue dress, was sitting in the studio, where she could see both the window and the clock. Anne, by the fire, was watching her.

'You seem very fairly calm, Hyacinth.'

'I am calm,' she said. 'I am; quite calm. Except that my heart is beating so fast that I can hardly breathe, that I have horrible kinds of shivers and a peculiar feeling in my throat, I'm quite all right. Now, just fancy if I had to pretend I wasn't in suspense! If I had no-one to confide in!... Do you think he's mistaken the day? Do you think he thinks it's Thursday instead of Tuesday?'

'That's not likely.'

'I'm glad I feel so cool and calm. How ashamed I should be if he ever knew that I was so agitated!'

'Who knows, perhaps he's feeling as uncomfortable as you are?'

'Oh, no, no! There's no hope of that.... Will he telephone and put it off, do you think, at the last minute?'

'I shouldn't think so.'

'Are there any little pink cakes?'

'Heaps. Far more than will ever be eaten.'

'Now, don't talk to me, Anne. I'm going to read for a quarter of an hour.'

She took up a novel and read two pages, then looked up at the clock and turned pale.

'It's five. Is that clock fast?'

'No; listen, the church clock's striking. Good-bye.'

Anne went, and Hyacinth kissed her hand to her and arranged her hair in the mirror. She then sat down and resolved to be perfectly quiet.

Ten minutes slowly ticked away, then Hyacinth went to the window, saying to herself that it was an unlucky thing to do. She did not remain there long, then walked round and round the room. Several cabs passed, each of which she thought was going to stop. Then she sat down again, looking cool and smiling, carelessly holding a book....

Each time the cab passed. It was half-past five, rather late under the circumstances. She was angry. She resolved to be very cold to him when he first came in, or—no, she wouldn't be cold, she would pretend she didn't know he was late—hadn't noticed it; or she would chaff him about it, and say she would never wait again. She took the letter from her pocket and read it again. It said:—

'DEAR MISS VERNEY, 'May I come and see you at five o'clock tomorrow afternoon?

'Yours,

'CECIL REEVE.'

Its very brevity had shown it was something urgent, but perhaps he would come to break off their friendship; since the awkwardness of Lady Cannon's visit, he must have been thinking that things couldn't go on like this. Then she began to recapitulate details, arguing to herself with all the cold, hard logic of passion.

At Lord Selsey's afternoon she had given herself away by her anger, by the jealousy she showed, and had told him never to come and see her again. Immediately after that had been their meeting at the National Gallery, where Cecil had followed her and sought her out. Then they had those two delightful walks in Kensington Gardens, in which he had really seemed to 'like' her so much. Then the pleasant intimate little lunch, after which Lady Cannon had called…. In the course of these meetings he had told her that he and Mrs Raymond had quarrelled, that she would never see him again. She had felt that he was drifting to her…. How strangely unlike love affairs in books hers had been! In all respectable novels it was the man who fell in love first. No-one knew by experience better than Hyacinth how easily that might happen, how very often it did. But she, who was proud, reserved, and a little shy with all her expansiveness, had simply fallen hopelessly in love with him at first sight. It was at that party at the Burlingtons. She realised now that she had practically thought of nothing else since. Probably she was spoilt, for she had not foreseen any difficulty; she had had always far more admirers than she cared for, and her difficulties had usually been in trying to get rid of them. He seemed to like her, but that was all. Mrs Raymond was, of course, the reason, but Mrs Raymond was over. She looked up at the clock again.

Ten minutes to six. Perhaps he had made it up with Mrs Raymond?… For the next ten minutes she suffered extraordinary mental tortures, then her anger consoled her a little. He had treated her too rudely! It was amazing—extraordinary! He was not worth caring for. At any rate, it showed he didn't care for her…. If it was some unavoidable accident, couldn't he have telephoned or telegraphed?… No; it was one of those serious things that one can only write about. He was with Mrs Raymond, she felt sure of that. But Mrs Raymond didn't like him…. Perhaps, after all, he had only been detained in some extraordinary way, she might hear directly….

She went up to her room, and was slightly consoled for the moment to find the clock there five minutes slower than the one in the drawing-room. She again arranged her hair and went into the hall, where she found two or three cards of people who had called, and been told she was out—an irritating detail—for nothing! Then she went back to the studio.

Even to be in the place where she had been waiting for him was something, it gave her a little illusion that he would be here again…. Could he really be an hour and a quarter late? It was just possible.

She heard a ring. Every sign of anxiety disappeared from her face. She was beaming, and got back into the old attitude, holding the book. She could hear her heart beating while there was some parley in the hall. Unable to bear it any more, she opened the door. It was someone with a parcel.

'What is it?'

'It's only the new candle-shades, miss. Shall I bring them in for you to see?'

'No, thank you….' Candle-

shades!

She put her hands over her eyes and summoned all her pride. Probably the very butler and her maid knew perfectly well she had been waiting at home alone for Mr Reeve. She cared absolutely nothing what they thought; but she felt bitter, revengeful to him. It was cruel.

Why did she care so much? She remembered letters and scenes with other people—people whose sufferings about her she felt always inclined to laugh at. She couldn't believe in it. Love in books had always seemed to her, although intensely interesting, just a trifle absurd. She couldn't realise it till now.

Another ring. Perhaps it was he after all! …

The same position. The book, the bright blue eyes….

The door opened; Anne came in. It was striking seven o'clock.

CHAPTER XVIII

Eugenia

Meanwhile Cecil had received a note from his uncle, asking him to go and see him. He decided he would do so on his way to see Hyacinth.

For many days now he had not seen Mrs Raymond. She had answered no letters, and been always 'out' to him.

As he walked along, he wondered what had become of her, and tried to think he didn't care.

'I have news for you, Cecil,' said his uncle; 'but, first, you really have made up your mind, haven't you, to try your luck with Hyacinth? What a pretty perfumed name it is—just like her.'

'I suppose I shall try.'

'Good. I'm delighted to hear it. Then in a very short time I shall hear that you're as happy as I am.'

'As you, Uncle Ted?'

'Look at this house, Cecil. It's full of Things; it wants looking after. I want looking after…. I am sure you wouldn't mind—wouldn't be vexed to hear I was going to marry again?'

'Rather not. I'm glad. It must be awfully lonely here sometimes. But I am surprised, I must say. Everybody looks upon you as a confirmed widower, Uncle Ted.'

'Well, so I have been a confirmed widower—for eighteen years. I think that's long enough.'

Cecil waited respectfully. Then his uncle

said abruptly—

'I saw Mrs Raymond yesterday.' Cecil

started and blushed.

'Did you? Where did you meet her?'

'I didn't meet her. I went to see her. I spent two hours with her.'

Cecil stared in silent amazement.

'It was my fourth visit,' said Lord Selsey.

'You spent all that time talking over my affairs?'

His uncle gave a slight smile. 'Indeed not, Cecil. After the first few minutes of the first visit, frankly, we said very little about you.'

'But I don't understand.'

'I've been all this time trying to persuade her to something—against her judgement. I've been trying to persuade her to marry.'

'To marry me?'

'No. To marry me. And I've succeeded.'

'I congratulate you,' said Cecil, in a cold, hard voice.

'You're angry, my boy. It's very natural; but let me explain to you how it happened.'

He paused, and then went on: 'Of course, for years I've wished for the right woman here. But I never saw her. I thought I never should. That day she came here—the musical party—the moment I looked at her, I saw that she was meant for me, not for you.'

'I call it a beastly shame,' said Cecil.

'It isn't. It's absolutely right. You know perfectly well she never would have cared for you in the way you wished.'

Cecil could not deny that, but he said sarcastically— 'So you fell

in love with her at first sight?'

'Oh no, I didn't. I'm not in love with her now. But I think she's beautiful. I mean she has a beautiful soul—she has atmosphere, she has something that I need. I could live in the same house with her in perfect harmony for ever. I could teach her to understand my Things. She does already by instinct.'

'You're marrying her as a kind of custodian for your collection?'

'A great deal, of course. And, then, I couldn't marry a young girl. It would be ridiculous. A society woman—a regular beauty—would jar on me and irritate me. She would think herself more important than my pictures.'

Cecil could hardly help a smile, angry as he was.

'And Mrs Raymond,' went on Lord Selsey, 'is delightfully unworldly—and yet sensible. Of course, she's not a bit in love with me either. But she likes me awfully, and I persuaded her. It was all done by argument.'

'I could never persuade her,' said Cecil bitterly.

'Of course not. She has such a sense of form. She saw the incongruity…. I needn't ask you to forgive me, old boy. I know, of course, there's nothing to forgive. You've got over your fancy, or you will very soon. I haven't injured you in any sort of way, and I didn't take her away from you. She's ten years older than you, and nine years younger than me…. You're still my heir just the same. This will make no difference, and you'll soon be reconciled. I'm sure of that.'

'Of course, I'm not such a brute as not to be glad, for her,' said Cecil slowly, after a slight struggle. 'It seems a bit rough, though, at first.' He held out his hand.

'Thanks, dear old boy. You see I'm right. You can't be angry with me…. You see it's a peculiar case. It won't be like an ordinary marriage, a young married couple and so on, nor a *mariage de convenance*, either, in the ordinary sense. Here are two lonely people intending to live solitary lives. Suddenly, you—*most* kindly, I must say—introduce us. I, with my great experience and my instinctive *flair*, see immediately that this is the right woman in the right place. I bother her until she consents—and there you are.'

'I hope you'll be happy.'

They shook hands in silence, and Cecil got into a hansom and drove straight to Mrs Raymond's. He was furious.

While Hyacinth, whose very existence he had forgotten in the shock and anger of this news, was feeling, with the agonising clairvoyance of love, that Cecil was with Mrs Raymond, she was perfectly right.

Today Eugenia was at home, and did not refuse to see him. 'I see you

know,' she remarked coolly as he came in.

Cecil had controlled his emotion when with his uncle, but seeing Mrs Raymond again in the dismal little old drawing-room dealt him a terrible blow. He saw, only too vividly, the picture of his suave, exquisite uncle, standing out against this muddled, confused background, in the midst of

decoration which was one long disaster and furniture that was one desperate failure. To think that the owner of Selsey House had spent hours here! The thought was jealous agony.

'I must congratulate you,' he said coldly. 'Thank you,

Cecil.'

'I thought you were never going to marry again?' he said sarcastically.

'I never do, as a rule. But this is an exception. And it isn't going to be like an ordinary marriage. We shall each have complete freedom. He persuaded me—to look after that lovely house. It will give me an object in life. And besides, Cecil,' she was laughing, 'think—to be your aunt! The privilege!'

He seized her by the shoulders. She laughed still more, and put one hand on the bell, at which he released her. He walked away so violently that he knocked down a screen.

'There, that will do,' said Eugenia, picking it up. 'You've made your little scene, and shown your little temper, and that's enough. Sit down,' she commanded.

Cecil sat down, feeling a complete fool.

'Look here. I daresay that it's a little annoying for you, at first, especially as you introduced us; but really, when you come to think it over, there's no law of etiquette, or any other that I know of, which compels me to refuse the uncle of a young man who has done me the honour to like me. Oh, Cecil, don't be absurd!'

'Are you in love with him?'

'No. But I think he will be very pleasant—not worrying and fidgeting—so calm and kind. I refused at first, Cecil. People always want what they can't get, and if it's any satisfaction to you, I don't mind confessing that I have had, for years, a perfect mania for somebody else. A hopeless case for at least three reasons: he's married, he's in love with someone else (not even counting his wife, who counts a great deal) and, if he hadn't either of these preoccupations, he would never look at me. So I've given it up. I've made up my mind to forget it. Your uncle will help me, and give me something else to think about.'

'Who was the man?' Cecil asked. It was some slight satisfaction to know that she also had had a wasted affection.

'Why should I tell you? I shall not tell you. Well, I will tell you. It's Sir Charles Cannon.'

'Old Cannon?'

'Yes; it was a sort of mad hero-worship. I never could account for it. I always thought him the most wonderful person. He hasn't the faintest idea of it, and never will; and now don't let's speak of him again.'

The name reminded Cecil of Hyacinth. He started violently, remembering his appointment. What must she have thought of him?

'Good-bye, Eugenia,' he said.

As he held her hand he felt, in a sense, as if it was in some strange way, after all, a sort of triumph for him, a score that Lord Selsey had appreciated her so wonderfully.

As he left the house it struck seven. What was he to do about Hyacinth?

That evening Hyacinth received a large basket of flowers and a letter, in which Cecil threw himself on her mercy, humbling himself to the earth, and imploring her to let him come and explain and apologise next day. He entreated her to be kind enough to let him off waiting till a conventional hour, and to allow him to call in the morning.

He received a kind, forgiving answer, and then spent the most miserable night of his life.

CHAPTER XIX

Bruce has Influenza

All women love news of whatever kind; even bad news gives them merely a feeling of pleasurable excitement, unless it is something that affects them or those they love personally.

Edith was no exception to the rule, but she knew that Bruce, on the contrary, disliked it; if it were bad he was angry and said it served the people right, while if it were good he thought they didn't deserve it and disapproved strongly. Bruce spent a great deal of his time and energy in disapproving; generally of things and people that were no concern of his. As is usually the case, this high moral attitude was caused by envy.

Bruce would have been much surprised to hear it, but envy was the keynote of his character, and he saw everything that surrounded him through its vague mist.

All newspapers made him furious. He regarded everything in them as a personal affront; from the fashionable intelligence, describing political dinners in Berkeley Square or dances in Curzon Street, where he thought he should have been present in the important character of host, to notices of plays—plays which he felt he could have written so well. Even sensational thefts irritated him; perhaps he unconsciously fancied that the stolen things (Crown jewels, and so forth) should by rights have been his, and that he would have known how to take care of them. 'Births, Marriages, and Deaths' annoyed him intensely. If he read that Lady So- and-So had twin sons, the elder of whom would be heir to the title and estates, he was disgusted to think of the injustice that he hadn't a title and estates for Archie to inherit, and he mentally held the newly-arrived children very cheap, feeling absolutely certain that they would compare most unfavourably with his boy, excepting, of course, in the accident of their worldly circumstances. Also, although he was proud of having married, and fond of Edith, descriptions of 'Society Weddings of the Week' drove him absolutely wild—wild to think that he and Edith, who deserved it, hadn't had an Archbishop, choirboys, guardsmen with crossed swords to walk under, and an amethyst brooch from a member of the Royal Family at their wedding. New discoveries in science pained him, for he knew that he would have thought of them long before, and carried them out much better, had he only had the time.

Bruce had had influenza, and when Edith came in with her news, she could not at once make up her mind to tell him, fearing his anger.

He was lying on the sofa with the paper, grumbling at the fuss made about the Sicilian players, of whom he was clearly jealous.

She sat down by his side and agreed with him.

'I'm much worse since you went out. You know the usual results of influenza, don't you? Heart failure, or nervous depression liable to lead to suicide.'

'But you're much better, dear. Dr Braithwaite said it was wonderful how quickly you threw it off.'

'Threw it off! Yes, but that's only because I have a marvellous constitution and great will-power. If I happened to have had less strength and vitality, I might easily have been dead by now. I wish you'd go and fetch me some cigarettes, dear. I have none left.'

She got up and went to the door.

'What are you fidgeting about, Edith?' said he. '*Can't* you keep still? It's not at all good for a convalescent to have a restless person with him.'

'Why, I was only going to fetch—'

'I know you were; but you should learn repose, dear. First you go out all the morning, and when you come home you go rushing about the room.'

She sat down again and decided to tell him.

'You'll be glad to hear,' she said, 'that Hyacinth and Cecil Reeve are engaged. They are to be married in the autumn.'

Guessing she expected him to display interest, he answered irritably— 'I don't

care. It has nothing to do with me.'

'No, of course not.'

'I never heard anything so idiotic as having a wedding in the autumn. A most beastly time, I think—November fogs.'

'I heard something else,' said Edith, 'which surprised me much more. Fancy, Lord Selsey's going to be married—to Mrs Raymond. Isn't that extraordinary?'

'Lord Selsey—a widower! Disgusting! I thought he pretended to be so fond of his first wife.'

'He was, dear, I believe. But she died eighteen years ago, and—'

'Instead of telling me all this tittle-tattle it would be much better if you did as I asked you, Edith, and fetched me the cigarettes. I've asked you several times. Of course I don't want to make a slave of you. I'm not one of those men who want their wives to be a drudge. But, after all, they're only in the next room. It isn't a *very* hard task! And I'm very weak, or I'd go myself.'

She ran out and brought them back before he could stop her again. 'Who is this

Mrs Raymond?' he then asked.

'Oh, she's a very nice woman—a widow. Really quite suitable in age to Lord Selsey. Not young. She's not a bit pretty and not in his set at all. He took the most violent fancy to her at first sight, it seems. She had vowed never to marry again, but he persuaded her.'

'Well,' said Bruce, striking a match, 'they didn't consult me! They must go their own way. I'm sorry for them, of course. Lord Selsey always seemed to me a very agreeable chap, so it seems rather a pity. At the same time, I suppose it's a bad thing—in the worldly sense—for Reeve, and *that's* satisfactory.'

'Oh! I think he's all right, said Edith, and she smiled thoughtfully.

'You're always smiling, Edith,' he complained. 'Particularly when I have something to annoy me.'

'Am I? I believe I read in the "Answers to Correspondents" in *Home Chirps* that a wife should always have a bright smile if her husband seemed depressed.'

'Good heavens! How awful! Why, it would be like living with a Cheshire cat!'

Edith warmly began to defend herself from the accusation, when Bruce stopped her by saying that his temperature had gone up, and asking her to fetch the clinical thermometer.

Having snatched it from her and tried it, he turned pale and said in a hollow voice—

'Telephone to Braithwaite. At once. Say it's urgent. Poor little Edith!'

'What is it?' she cried in a frightened voice.

'I'd better not tell you,' he said, trying to hide it. 'Tell me—

oh! tell me!'

'It's a hundred and nineteen. Now don't waste time. You meant no harm, dear, but you worried and excited me. It isn't your fault. Don't blame yourself. Of course, you *would* do it.'

'Oh, I know what it is,' cried Edith. 'I dipped it in boiling water before I gave it to you.'

'Idiot! You might have broken it!' said Bruce.

The explanation seemed to annoy him very much; nevertheless he often referred afterwards to the extraordinary way his temperature used to jump about, which showed what a peculiarly violent, virulent, dangerous form of influenza he had had, and how wonderful it was he had thrown it off, in spite of Edith's inexperienced, not to say careless, nursing, entirely by his own powerful will and indomitable courage.

Made in the USA
Middletown, DE
12 November 2017